GODS

IN THE GAME

Messages on the Awakening and Consciousness Shift

ALEX MARCOUX

In co-creation with Shauna Kalicki, Daniel, and Connie

Gods In the Game: Messages on the Awakening
and Consciousness Shift
By Alex Marcoux, with Shauna Kalicki, Daniel, and Connie

To request permission, contact the publisher at jenness333@gmail.com.

Paperback: 978-1-7352611-0-2
Library of Congress Number: 2023922042

First paperback edition

Edited by Donna Mazzitelli, Writing With Donna
Proofreading by Jennifer Bisbing
Cover art and layout by Victoria Wolf, wolfdesignandmarketing.com
Cover image by Josie Yerby

Printed in the USA.
616 Editions, an Imprint of Jenness

616 Editions

P.O. Box 620681
Littleton, CO 80162

To all those awakening and the awakened—
this book is for you. Thank you for your service.

OTHER BOOKS BY ALEX MARCOUX

Nonfiction

Destination New Earth: A Blueprint to 5D Consciousness
Lifesigns: Tapping the Power of Synchronicity,
Serendipity and Miracles

Novels

The Unsuspected Heroes: A Visionary Fiction Novel
A Matter of Degrees
Back to Salem
Facades

Contributing Author

50 Great Writers You Should be Reading
Awakening and Applying Intuition and Psychic Ability

CONTENTS

FOREWORD

Life is a game.
To move on to the next level, one must listen with their
heart, live authentically, and be a lion, not a lamb.

IN OUR PREVIOUS BOOK, *Destination New Earth,* Daniel the
Ethereal Autist added a message to his mother Connie's foreword.
It was "Welcome home." She interpreted it as welcoming the
reader to the New Earth and letting that book guide them.

In the same spirit, I asked Daniel if he wanted to give an introduction and closing message for this book. One day, I received a note
for the foreword. It was also two words, "dead game."

In case you haven't read *Destination New Earth,* in it we reveal
that life is a game, and there are various levels or rounds to the
game. The 3D, third dimension, objective is to awaken to your
Divine Blueprint and live your Truth. Mother Mary shared, "The
game is to live the blueprint written for you long ago before you
incarnated. Every individual must live their Truth, their higher
self, their blueprint."

The third-dimension objective is to "BE." We are going through
a dimensional shift in consciousness. Some refer to it as a shift from

3D to 5D (third dimension to fifth dimension). There is also a unique objective in 5D, which we explore further in this book.

When asking Daniel to expand on his message of "dead game," this is what he wrote:

> "Think of it as going into a new phase. The game is coming to an end. The next step in our evolution has new rules, new twists and turns. People will be more interactive and not trying to defeat each other. The idea is the game will die, and there will be more cooperation. Shift over into a new way of thinking."

Think of this as if we're playing a game, and the 3D level concludes. We are to move on, if we choose, to the next level. The 3D deconstructs, and a new round emerges with new rules.

Daniel shared that he'd provide more information as humanity becomes ready to hear it and that it needs to be shared with humankind in phases to understand it. He did say, "Be open to new possibilities because the game is over."

Before I had an opportunity to receive more information from Daniel, I visited with Shauna Kalicki, a channel for many beings, including Cerian, a sixteenth-dimensional collective. While Shauna channeled Cerian, I asked them if they knew what Daniel meant by "dead game."

They added, "From our perspective, when the game is dead, that would mean humanity has awakened and are in unison. They would be aware that they're creators and co-creators, and the few no longer control the many—the many control the few. That's the illusion. No one individual or group of people can control others. The game would be over when there's no veil."

That certainly is *not* where we are today, but I believe it is where we are heading.

Cerian further indicated that the 3D level is ending, and we are starting a transition period. This period is what Daniel referred to.

Daniel mentioned, "There is this level of acceptance in the collective of humanity of the world's craziness. The Shades are still manipulating and creating pockets of chaos around the globe. Humans are almost used to it, and this creates an environment of 'heavenly coherence.'"

There has been a level of control over humankind since the beginning in Lemuria. This control continued and became the norm with the Controllers, or Shades, as Daniel puts it. The Controllers became the establishment, as reflected in the uneven distribution of wealth worldwide.

There is undoubtedly much craziness and chaos in the outer world—war, hunger, "natural disasters," corruption, global warming, an accelerated level of violence, human trafficking, systems collapsing, epidemics, and more. Because of this, there is also a new level of fear in the inner world.

Daniel is suggesting that much of humanity continues to do what they have always done: follow the establishment mindlessly. Since the beginning, to survive, humankind wanted someone to lead, so we followed the Controllers and still do in 2024.

You are a sovereign being, though you don't remember, and if you surrender your sovereignty, you choose not to be the Creator that you are and create with haphazard results. When giving over your divine sovereign right, you create unconsciously. You choose destabilization, instead of stabilization, enlightenment, growth, awareness, and awakening.

So, as light is shined on the Controllers and their minions, and the darkness and corruption of the Shades are exposed, humanity has a choice to either make the Controllers and their minions accountable or look the other way as society has done in the past.

The Controllers are in a fragile state and are losing their grip on control; though, as Daniel suggests, they are still creating chaos worldwide.

Because humans have become so desensitized to senseless behavior, many choose the consistency of the establishment. Like sheep, they follow, considering thought and reason rather than listening to their hearts, and by doing so, they surrender their sovereignty.

Daniel suggests that some groups working for the Light Team are taking advantage of this period, which has "less fight energy." It permits "secret missions to go down under their noses without the Shades seeing it."

To put it simply, the Controllers have had better days. They're getting hit by the efforts of the Autist Collective, a network of Pure Autists working around the planet to awaken humanity.

Daniel later said, "The control will die."

From my perspective, both Daniel's and Cerian's messages make sense and offer much hope, given that humanity is on the verge of an evolutionary shift. To advance the 3D level, we must live our authentic selves and enter a new phase with new rules and goals. Rather than sheep, we must be the lion and listen with our hearts. Newness often accompanies uncertainty, and uncertainty accompanies chaos. There seems to be much of that in the outer world right now.

Life is a game with various levels, and as the 3D round is deconstructing, a new level emerges. To move on, one must listen to their heart, live their authentic self, and be the lion, not the lamb.

Know that if you are here to awaken and have not learned about your Divine Blueprint or sovereignty, it is not too late. May *Gods in the Game* and *Destination New Earth* help you on your path through this transition period and onward to the 5D level of the game.

Blessings,
Alex Marcoux

ACKNOWLEDGMENTS

I AM GRATEFUL TO THE Light Team members who said *yes* to being frontline unsung heroes in this shift in consciousness. If you were drawn to read this book, you are likely among the members. We have a thankless job, yet that is why we are here. What you do with the material in this book is unknown. It may rattle your cage. It may trigger an awakening. I hope you read it with an open heart and mind and take what resonates. It is also my hope that you share this book with those of like mind so that it can reach those it needs to reach. Know that you are loved beyond measure, and Mother Mary adds, "Now is the time to own your magnificence, for you truly are the Light within this world."

I cannot begin to express my thanks to the co-creators of this book, Shauna Kalicki, Connie, and Daniel, for their willingness to roll up their sleeves and dive in so that we could bring this information to the world. Each made substantial sacrifices for this project; I couldn't have created this book without them. I value their efforts but, more importantly, our friendship and their love, and I love each of them dearly.

This book would not have been possible without Cerian, Mother Mary, Daniel, unnamed spiritual guides, and the Autist Collective, who entrusted me with the information and guided me to bring it forward in this format so you can read it.

I want to thank my production team, who all exceeded my expectations and took great care of the work: Donna Mazzitelli and Jennifer Bisbing for editing, and Victoria Wolf for design and layout.

I also must acknowledge the magnificent work of the artist Josie Yerby and her painting, "Queen of the Night," which spoke to me in the Eureka Springs gift store. After bringing the art home, it wanted a place on the cover. To me, it is reminiscent of Sophia.

I cannot express enough gratitude for my nearly forty-year friendship with Susan, who recently transitioned from earth and was one of my most significant teachers.

For my son, I am grateful for his love and support. To my family, Team Blue Ray, and friends, those named and unnamed, who have supported me in this journey, you are my heroes, and I love you all.

For Sophia, the Cosmic C, Source Consciousness, thank you for permitting me a seat at the table so I can be of service.

PREFACE

When we show up for God—God shows up for us.

ABOUT SIX MONTHS AFTER *Destination New Earth* was published, I sat down to write another book—this book. It was to be a sort of bridge book. One that could help a person new to the spiritual path better understand *Destination New Earth*. A month later, I was well over a hundred pages into that book when I visited with Shauna Kalicki, Daniel, and Connie, contributors to *Destination New Earth*. Shauna is the psychic medium who channels Cerian, the Ascended Masters, and Daniel.

During that reunion, Daniel shared a piece of writing with me. It was good—a bit edgy and controversial, but Truth. It was right up my alley. I have always sought out and revealed hidden Truths to the world. That's what I did in *Destination New Earth*, *The Unsuspected Heroes*, and all my other books, though unknowingly at the time. It is something I feel I am to do while I'm here.

I asked Daniel if I could share his insights in the new book I had been writing. Daniel, a nonspeaking autistic man, typed, "Yes." But I had many questions about what he shared, which was a written dialogue between Connie and him on God.

1

During this reunion with the *Destination New Earth* team, Shauna Kalicki and I planned to get together the following month and explore many of my questions in channeling sessions. I wanted to bring in the wisdom of Cerian and Mother Mary, similar to how we worked on *Destination New Earth*.

Before Shauna and I met, Daniel had sent other material to me and shared that he wanted to convey three messages to humanity. The first, as mentioned, was on God. The second was on Lemuria, and I hesitate to say the third, but we will get to that.

On our first channeling, I asked how readers were reacting to *Destination New Earth*. It wasn't easy to gauge how readers were doing with the material and if it was doing what the "higher-ups" wanted it to do. That book was a leap of faith for me, and the information relayed was not exactly warm and fuzzy like most spirituality books.

About the book, Cerian, the sixteenth-dimension collective speaking through one voice, said, "We are very pleased to say it is doing exactly what we had hoped it would do. It draws in individuals who may be able to resonate with the information within the book. It is startling some, awakening others, and pushing buttons in others. This is good. We want to be dramatic in many respects about what is happening."

When Cerian says "what is happening," they are talking about the planetary shift in consciousness and the awakening of humanity.

"So, it is doing exactly as it should and will continue to grow and expand over the years," Cerian said. "And this delights us as the energy and the information are moving out into the world."

Destination New Earth is energy. Everything is energy, and everything is connected.

"The energetic code is bringing to light the subjects you have brought up in your book," Cerian continued. "Those subjects have a frequency. How you address them in your book has a unique frequency within that book. By having that out in the consciousness of humanity, those energetic codes are being received. They are triggering people. They are opening people. They are awakening people, and so, it is a codebook."

Cerian agreed that the sequencing and frequency of words might be thought of as codes or symbolism, but the genuine power in *Destination New Earth: A Blueprint to 5D Consciousness* is the energetic codes.

"It is the messaging about the topics regarding humanity's sovereignty, Divine Blueprint, taking responsibility for what people create, the encouragement for people to question what's going on in your world at this point about COVID, the light side, the spiritual war, the light, and dark.

"The information was needed to be out in the consciousness of humanity. It is a slow trickle at this point, as it should be. There needs to be time to get humanity's consciousness, awareness, and energetic fields up where they can work with and handle this energy."

This passage from Cerian was reminiscent of what Daniel shared. He mentioned that humanity has what one may think of as a black sludge around our heads that keeps us wanting to self-destruct. It can be cleaned up or healed, but if it occurs too quickly, it will be too disorienting to humanity, so it has to be "a slow trickle."

Consider books like *Gods in the Game* and *Destination New Earth* as part of this "slow trickle" to clear that black sludge so we can heal and awaken to the truths hidden from humanity.

My questions posed for this book were in three sets of channeling sessions. At the end of the first group of channelings, it was the Ascended Master Mother Mary who showed me that the questions I had posed in channelings did not align with the original intention, which was to write a bridge book for someone new on the spiritual path.

Mother Mary said, "We recognize in these questions that they are not basic. The topics are much more complex than a very gentle bridging book. A bridging book brings people into the concept—you are Spirit within a physical form and can make choices, be sovereign, and explore that concept. Many of the children that are coming into the world are already aware of this. For them, *Destination New Earth* will make sense. But some children coming into the world do not have that awareness."

Mother Mary explained that the concepts of souls, oversouls, God, and Divine Blueprints are far beyond many readers, particularly those reading a bridge book. She even said the idea of creation that humanity currently is being fed is "much more basic than what is true."

When sharing that I wanted to reach readers to help awaken them and provide a sort of *Destination New Earth* 101 book, she discouraged simplifying the concepts we had discussed. Mother Mary then listed several topics we spoke of in the sessions for this book and *Destination New Earth* and said, "These are still very bold concepts for those who are awakened."

She encouraged me to continue writing to those who are awakening or have awakened. So, I considered Mother Mary's words and said, "Maybe it's about expanding the ideas within *Destination New Earth* rather than simplifying them for a bridge book."

"We're seeing light around that," Mother Mary responded. "There is energy around the expansion of *Destination New Earth*."

And so, that is what I have done. This book is for those who are awakening and those who are awakened.

INTRODUCTION

"I have said, ye are Gods." —Psalms 82:6 (KJV)
Some say it is blasphemy to think you're God.
It's blasphemous to think otherwise.

THIS BOOK IS NOT FOR EVERYONE. It is not a spirituality book for beginners nor a prayer book. It is not visionary fiction. It's not solely a spiritual memoir, but you may call it a spiritual memoir "plus" the insights of higher-dimensional beings.

This book is nonfiction and intended for readers who are awakening or awakened during our current planetary shift in consciousness. It is for the *awakened* and *awakening* Lightworkers, Starseeds, 144000, Wayshowers, New Children, Autists, and the Awakened Ones. It is for the Light Team.

Much of the information within *Gods in the Game* is channeled by Shauna Kalicki and from the Ascended Master Mother Mary, the Ethereal Autist Daniel, and Cerian. I'm the first to admit that information from twelfth-dimension Mother Mary, sixteenth-dimension Cerian, and the all-dimensional Daniel does not always agree. But that shouldn't be surprising; everyone comes from a different—not higher or lower—point of reference, including me.

What makes this channeled material different from some other books is that I am not the channel. The channel is Shauna Kalicki. I discern the channeled material through my set of filters, always intending to write and reveal the Truth.

Please know that I am a fellow journeyer, writer, and intuitive. If you have read my earlier work, you know I strive to reveal Truths that have been lost or hidden from humanity. I consider myself the interviewer and, in many cases, the interpreter of the information. Still, as you will see, much of the material is given in its original dialogue, especially if it could be interpreted in many ways.

At times, I provide both the channeled information and follow with my interpretation of it. Not because I want to be repetitive or put in my two cents, but because I am not perfect, and your interpretation may take you elsewhere—which is good. I do not want to hinder your experience, but add to it where I can.

Other times, when the messages are evident to me, yet the language of the channeled entity is complex, I break down the messages and paraphrase them to help make the reading experience easier.

Gods in the Game is a standalone book. As I indicated in the preface, this book expands on the concepts presented in *Destination New Earth*. I do not want you to feel you *have to* read *Destination New Earth* first. Admittedly, though, I hope you're inspired to read it after this book because it is energetically a boosting experience in itself.

Parts I and II of this book either serve as a refresher for the *Destination New Earth* reader or summarize portions of that book for those who haven't read it. Those two sections cover autism's role in the evolutionary shift and provide essential information on the New Earth so we can expand on certain concepts in the later sections.

In Part III, I dive into the various types and stages of awakening that humanity experiences and discuss a higher level of awakening that the planet needs now to jumpstart a collective evolutionary shift.

I also discuss the difference between awakening, enlightenment, and ascension.

The later parts of the book jump into topics that Daniel wanted to discuss. He had particular messages for humanity about God, and in his words, "It is a fabric of reality that is completely unknown to humans. Humans are only scratching the surface." He also wanted to talk about Lemuria and sovereignty and the state of the planet. I explored these topics further with Cerian and Mother Mary.

Some of the "what-if" prompts explored within *Gods in the Game* include:

- What if you manifest and create your life from the perspective of energy?
- What if you created your own world, and no one else is responsible for it but you?
- What if you made choices—you wrote your storyline and are constantly writing your storyline—and nobody else is except you?
- What if there is a Spark of Life within you, and you have the potential to access the Spark of Light within, which is God Consciousness?
- What if you can work with that God Consciousness if you choose to be responsible or accountable for your own life and thoughts?
- What if the cream of the crop, those awakened Lightworkers, Starseeds, 144000, New Children, and others, were to experience the ascension right now? Do you think that is why you're here?
- What if I told you that you're not here to ascend but to experience an evolutionary collective shift in consciousness?

- What if I told you—*you* are a God in the game?
- What if I told you that humans created God?

I hear the cries of, "Blasphemy, heresy, sacrilege!"

Didn't Yeshua (Jesus) say, "I have said, Ye are gods; and all of you are children of the most High" (Psalms 82:6 (KJV)). In this case, isn't it more blasphemous to think otherwise?

Let me add one more "what if." What if God shows up for us when we show up for God?

My interest has always been to help readers understand these concepts. Since each reader is not at the same point in their spiritual journey, whether I write fiction or nonfiction, I provide a glossary of terms at the back of my books and online at my website (alexmarcoux.com/ascension-glossary). We are all on different paths, and I don't want to lose anyone. I encourage you to refer to the glossary when unfamiliar with my terms.

Since 2011, I have been learning about what this book calls "Pure Autism." Who are the Pure Autists? Certainly, *Destination New Earth* shares more, but to simplify, let's just say they are higher energetic beings. I've devoted over a decade to learning from them, studying, and writing books like *The Unsuspected Heroes, Destination New Earth,* and now *Gods in the Game.*

Over the years, I've sensed that some spiritual teachers, particularly those asking to be followed, are not authentic. Yet, I've never felt inauthenticity with the Ethereal Autists I know. They have never asked to be followed nor demanded anything from anyone. They serve us and ask much from their families and caregivers to support them while doing their work, all because they love us.

I used fiction to communicate their stories in *The Unsuspected Heroes.* I chose that path because fiction hits the reader where they're at. If the reader is unawakened, they will read a story, and seeds will be planted. Those seeds may never germinate, but the reader could become more open to metaphysical concepts. If the reader is awakened, they will have an entirely different experience.

As in the earlier book, *Destination New Earth*, this information is not exactly warm and fuzzy. Some of it is downright controversial. But it is time to make it known to humanity. This book may resonate with you or it may challenge you. I ask that you read this with an open heart and mind—that is your job. My job has always been to convey the information that resonates as Truth.

PART I

Autism in a New Light

Chapter 1:

HOW TO COMMUNICATE WITH NONSPEAKING AUTISTICS

*Facilitated communication is training wheels
for the facilitator (not the Autist).*

FOR THOSE WHO HAVE NOT READ *Destination New Earth* and are not familiar with the role of autism in planetary ascension, this section will bring you up to speed. Otherwise, it will serve as a refresher.

I have personally met and worked with three Autists who are nonverbal, nonspeaking, or some suggest "beyond" verbal. They do not voice words. You may wonder, "How exactly do they communicate?"

Since Daniel was such a pivotal contributor to this book and our last book, I'll use him as an example. But understand that each Autist is different.

Daniel communicates using a supported typing method called FC (facilitated communication). In Daniel's case, he uses a plastic QWERTY letterboard. A facilitator, his mother, Connie, holds his hand and stabilizes it so that the movement is more pinpointed and accurate when he points to the letters to form words. When

Daniel messages in this manner, I show his written communication in a `different font` to demonstrate his letterboard communication.

I also have worked with Lyrica Marquez, the co-author of *AWEtizm* and *Lyrica's Journey of Ascension*. In Lyrica's case, she can point to a letterboard, computer keyboard, or tablet. But the principle is the same; the facilitator supports the autistic's hand or arm and sometimes provides ever-so-slight resistance so that the Autist "types" more accurately.

Daniel refers to this form of communication as training wheels. This method is very slow, and while people seem to think it may prove the autistic is actually communicating, it is the least favorite way for some autistics. Why? Energetically, it takes a lot out of them. Of course, I only speak for those I have met.

It's easier for Daniel, and the others, to convey more expansive topics, such as God, the planetary ascension, alternate dimensions, and the like, through psychic communications or telepathy. In both these methods, as in any psychic communication, the person communicating with Daniel must have a clean filter system to ensure accurate information. Another way Daniel shares is through Shauna Kalicki, the psychic medium.

A medium mediates communication between an individual and spirits or other-dimensional beings. Shauna is not a trance medium. She uses a mental form of mediumship where she is conscious. Rather than go into a trance, she opens to the communication—perhaps Cerian, Mother Mary, or Daniel—and conveys their messages. After the channeling, she often has a general sense of what came through, but the details sometimes get past her.

I have also witnessed Shauna channel many Ascended Masters over the years. Ascended Masters are those beings who lived in physicality (physical form) at one time and achieved the higher realms (ascended) in other lifetimes. You and I are now living in a physical form, though we are energetic beings.

When on a spiritual path, we strive to connect with our higher self or soul and embody that spiritual essence. We strive to integrate our soul's essence into our physical body.

Mother Mary ensured that "Humans can embody and carry that same energetic frequency [as their higher self]." There are risks with an Ethereal Autist embodying their complete essence, which I expand on later.

Some Ascended Masters I have witnessed Shauna channel are the Magdalenes, a secretive group within the Essenes, including Mother Mary, Mary Magdalene, Yeshua (Jesus), Anna (grandmother of Yeshua), and Joachim. The Magdalenes brought in a new awareness during Yeshua's lifetime, showing humanity that one can experience the higher self and sovereignty while in physicality. That is the work they did. That is the work we are now doing. During Yeshua's timeline, humanity was not ready as a collective to experience it.

I have also seen Shauna channel Archangel Metatron, Archangel Michael, and Cerian. In Cerian's case, the process is similar in scope to Carla L. Rueckert, who channeled the "I Am RA collective of sixth density" in the eighties, and Esther Hicks, who currently channels Abraham, "a group consciousness from the non-physical dimension."

For those not reading our earlier book, the reason Cerian was deemed by Daniel a "good channel" is because Shauna and Daniel both have expressions of their soul in the collective of Cerian.

What exactly does that mean?

Each person is multidimensional at the soul level. Our soul has multiple "lifetimes" or expressions co-occurring. Shauna's and Daniel's souls have a soul expression in the sixteenth dimension as part of the group known as Cerian. I call them "expressions" because they are not physical in the sixteenth dimension. They are purely energetic, ethereal, or spiritual. So, when Cerian speaks, they speak with the wisdom of multiple expressions through one voice.

How Did We Verify the Information?

What was exciting about working on *Destination New Earth* was that in using a combination of these methods (facilitated communication, telepathy, other psychic processes, channeling), we developed a unique approach to verify the accuracy of the information coming through in channeling sessions.

I would sit with Shauna privately in a channeling session, and she would bring in a being we wanted to communicate with. I would ask questions that Connie and I had prepared. Shauna did not see the questions before the channelings or even know the book's subject matter. The sessions were audio recorded.

After the sessions, I would send the recordings to Connie, who would transcribe them. Connie is also intuitive, and we would review the recordings, each adding levels of discernment, and develop follow-up questions for future sessions to clarify the information that had come through.

Connie would then read the channeling transcripts to Daniel, no matter who was channeled, and he would grade the accuracy of each response using FC. He also would add information with FC or suggest we ask other questions in future sessions.

While writing *Destination New Earth*, we learned early on how other beings can contaminate the information when, in one session, a trickster came in, claiming to be an angelic aspect of Daniel. This entity hijacked the session. The following day, I asked Connie to check if this angel was indeed who he claimed to be. It wasn't. Daniel cautioned that we must not use that material for the book. The channeling was never transcribed.

For this book, I was also given information from Daniel and Connie on messages he wanted to convey to humanity. This information mainly came from facilitated communication (FC). From these topics, I developed questions and asked whomever Shauna was channeling, either Cerian or Mother Mary. Connie assisted with transcribing, and Daniel monitored the transcription, ensuring a different entity hadn't hijacked the sessions.

Daniel had taken a significant role in *Destination New Earth* in that Shauna channeled him, and he became a considerable voice in that book. For this book, Cerian and Mother Mary spoke through Shauna, not Daniel, who communicated mostly through FC. However, given that an expression of Daniel's soul is one of those within the Cerian collective, Daniel's deeper insights are very present within these pages.

Chapter 2:

THE DEETS ON AUTISM

"No matter what, autism was supposed to happen. There are no accidents."
—Daniel

I AM THE FIRST TO ADMIT that I do not have a bunch of initials after my name, like PhD, MD, PsyD, VIP, or even DMin. My degree is not in psychiatry or psychology, and I'm not a minister. I am a student of life. I do not seek to be a "specialist," nor do I want to be followed. My role is to impart these teachings to help heal the planet because we all know that much needs to heal in this world.

Why listen to me? Over the years, those Autists I've met entrusted me with information and want me to bring their messages into the world. What has guided me through this process has been my inner guidance system, along with the encouragement of Autists and a small group I call my tribe.

Society says autism is a disorder.

Contemporary society witnesses autism and doesn't understand it. Autism makes people uncomfortable. It frightens people. When humanity doesn't understand something, humanity puts *it* in a box, and for autistics, that box is "autism." For the autistic, the stigma is feeling less than, unworthy, and not normal . . . unless they are awakened. I will get to that.

Merriam-Webster defines autism as *a variable developmental disorder that appears by age three and is characterized especially by difficulties in forming and maintaining social relationships, by impairment of the ability to communicate verbally or nonverbally, and by repetitive behavior patterns and restricted interests and activities.*

Merriam-Webster defines a "disorder" as *not functioning in a normal orderly healthy way.*

Merriam-Webster also defines a "species" as *a class of individuals having common attributes and designated by a common name.*

I am here to tell you that autism is a species by itself.

Lemuria was an ancient civilization predating Atlantis. Autist-like energy has existed on Earth since the Lemurians lived on Earth. I say "energy" because *everything is energy,* and we will get to that.

It is time to highlight the real definition of autism and eliminate the term ASD (autism spectrum disorder) because it is *not* a disorder.

If an individual is here to experience Pure Autism, it is part of their Divine Blueprint. They are here serving in a capacity few understand.

I am not taking away from the challenges that autistics experience because those challenges are real. Autistics experience life differently than what society calls a "normal" human being. Society requires autistics to overcome their challenges, fit in, adapt, and make everyone else feel more comfortable around them.

Why? Why does humanity require autistics to change their behavior so that people feel better about themselves? When will society be more tolerant and willing to accept individual differences rather than demand conforming? In reality, these beings have expanded consciousness and intelligence.

As of 2023, one in thirty-six children have autism.
If we go back forty years, according to the CDC, the incidence of autism was four in 10,000 children. That number today, based on the surveillance year 2020, is one in thirty-six. Why the increase? There are many theories, and I am not here to debate them. However, I will mention a few.

Some suggest that the rate has increased because of environmental factors, such as childhood vaccinations. Others argue parents are getting older when conceiving their children, and others claim that social and political factors favor an autism diagnosis over others.

I met Lyrica Marquez, the nonspeaking co-author of *AWEtizm*, in 2011, and after meeting her, plus having a science background, I was curious. I looked into the theories of the sudden increase back then. In my heart, none of the "theories" offered an explanation that resonated as truth. The following is what I learned from the channelings conducted for *Destination New Earth*.

Do childhood vaccinations cause autism?
There is some truth to vaccinations causing autism, but *not* in the way most would think.

If someone incarnates and it is in their Divine Blueprint to experience Pure Autism, the vaccinations will indeed *trigger* autism. Did it cause it? I guess that's up for debate. Because if they weren't vaccinated, something else would eventually activate it.

This information was indeed difficult for Connie to hear at first because when Daniel received his vaccinations, Connie saw Daniel slip away right after receiving the shots.

Daniel said that if the individual is here to experience Pure Autism, it will happen no matter what, and it is not an accident.

Vaccinations hurt some children.

Sadly, some children not destined for Pure Autism cannot absorb the inoculations and become damaged by them. They can become injured and brain damaged. Because their indicators resemble those behaviors of the Pure Autist, they get diagnosed with autism; however, they are not a Pure Autist if it's not in their soul assignment. We call those people hurt by vaccinations Medically Induced Autistics.

Why is the autism rate increasing?

The indication I got from the channelings was that the vaccinations didn't significantly cause the increase in autism rate. However, the vaccinations have hurt many children who cannot absorb the chemicals injected.

So why has the rate increased? It goes back to the battle between light and dark.

We are amid a spiritual evolution and revolution, and the Autists' work is needed on Earth today more than ever. More Autists will be incarnating and joining our society. When I wrote *Destination New Earth,* the autism rate based on the year 2016 was one in fifty-four. In four years, that's a 50 percent increase in the autism rate.

Scientists suggest the increase is because there is a growing awareness. That argument may hold when comparing data from 1980 to 2020 but *not* from 2016 to 2020. Don't you find this increase alarming? We will uncover the genuine reason for the increase later in the book.

In any case, Pure Autism is not a disorder. Pure Autists are brilliant, energetic, spiritual beings, a unique species, and here to assist humanity in its spiritual evolution.

Chapter 3:

A NEW SPECTRUM AND THE ROLE OF AUTISM IN THE SHIFT

*"No matter how limited or disabled the Autist
body is, our minds are completely free.
Most of the time, we Autists are aware
of our capacity to be free."*
—Daniel

IT'S TIME SOCIETY STARTS TO THINK of autism as different, not
less than; as a gift, not a reject; as intelligent, not brain damaged. It's
time to rename the spectrum; it is not the autism spectrum disorder (ASD) because it is not a developmental disorder. It's time to
understand the true scope of the diverse groups within the Autist
spectrum.

An Autist is an autistic person who knowingly or unknowingly
works on the planetary shift in consciousness, which is part of their
Divine Blueprint.

No matter where they fit on the new spectrum, all autistics are
part of a unique species experiencing life differently from aver-
age humans. Just like humanity has varying roles in this shift in
consciousness, so do the Autists. We all have a role to play.

The new spectrum has three distinct groups, though others may exist. The three groups within the Pure Autism Spectrum are the Ethereal Autists, Bridge Autists, and Catalytic Autists.

All three Autists I've worked with, Daniel, Lyrica, and Leilah, are Ethereal Autists. While *society* considers these beings low functioning, nonverbal, mentally retarded, and on the high end of the ASD, they have expanded consciousness and intelligence. Sometimes, I call these Pure Autists "Sacred Autists" because it feels fitting as their energy more closely aligns with Lemurian energy, and we will dive deep into that later.

The Ethereal Autist, AKA Pure Autist

To understand how the Ethereal Autists experience life, I compare them to humankind.

Humans are energetic beings who have a physical experience.

There is more to a human than a physical body, as we have a higher self or a soul. When humans are on a spiritual path, we strive to embody our energetic essence in our physical form (physicality) while retaining the connection with the soul.

It is important to understand that humans can embody or infuse the Light (Divine Energy) from their higher selves into their physical bodies. This process may be called by many names, including spiritual embodiment, shifting consciousness, dimensional shift, enlightenment, and awakening.

Ethereal Autists are energetic beings having an energetic experience.

The frequency of the Pure Autist energy is so high that they *cannot embody* all their essence because it would fry their circuits. Daniel shares, "The Pure Autist calibration of their energy and mind into physicality is like putting a jet engine on a go-cart." The Autist body can't handle the energy (the Light). So, the Ethereal Autists remain lightly tethered to their physical bodies. They are not entirely in their bodies and are experiencing other realities.

When someone looks at an autistic and concludes that "they aren't all there," that isn't far from the truth. But the psychiatric or medical conclusion implies that the autistic is impaired, not that these brilliant beings simply tend to matters elsewhere. Because the Autist is elsewhere, we see communication challenges and various behaviors that baffle us.

When you're distracted by something, are you all there? In your distractions, have you had communication challenges? Perhaps moments of clumsiness? Of course, you have. We all have.

The Ethereal Autist experiences life in an entirely different way from how humanity experiences life. They experience multidimensionality, other lifetimes, planets, and universes. Just as we can't imagine what it is like to have the ethereal experience, the Ethereal Autist cannot imagine what it is like to have a "normal" physical life. Their reality is seeing time and space. The Ethereal Autists have no veil obscuring their relationship with Source (God).

While the Ethereal Autist has challenges communicating with humans, they converse with other Autists in other realms. They communicate with the Ascended Masters, angels, galactic beings (yes—aliens), and other life-forms. Much of this communication is telepathic.

Bridge and Catalytic Autists

Two other groups within the Pure Autism Spectrum are the Bridge Autists and Catalytic Autists.

As the name implies, the Bridge Autists are more embodied than the Ethereal Autists and serve as a bridge between humanity and the higher realms and dimensions where the Ethereal Autists work. Given that they are more embodied and can manage better in their physical form, these autistics may have language skills and more control of their bodies. They serve us in ways we do not understand, and they may not understand either. They may be aware of their role in this shift, or they may not, depending on if they have awakened.

Catalytic Autists may be likened to those labeled with Asperger syndrome (AS) or Asperger's. They are generally considered high-functioning and on the low end of ASD by society's medical standards.

The Catalytic Autists understand how to participate in life and are in control of their bodies, unlike the Ethereal and Bridge Autists. Yet, they are still not fully integrated.

"These Autists work with specific energies that are creative catalysts to shift consciousness. Some of them are aware that they are doing this work. Others are unaware, but, in both cases, they assist humanity in ways society does not understand."[1]

The Autist Collective Consists of Silent Heroes

The Autist Collective consists of Ethereal Autists around the planet. Their work is to help awaken humanity. Humanity unknowingly has agreed to undergo an evolutionary shift, often called the New Earth. Autists have that awareness and hold that vision for the world and humanity.

Daniel says, "We hold the construct and infrastructure of the New Earth."

In truth, everything is energy, whether matter (solid, liquid, gas, plasma), thoughts, words, emotions, ether, and so on. *Everything* is energy. Everything has a frequency. The Pure Autists work with energy, and while they create situations to help us awaken to it and experience it, humanity needs to move with the energy and expectation that something bigger is coming in.

To do the work the Sacred Autists must do, they must remain nonjudgmental. This work is something humanity would not be able to do today because humans permit emotions to cloud their judgment. We use the labels "good" and "bad or "right" and "wrong." Everything and everyone has a role to play in the shift, and the Ethereal Autists can see the bigger picture and remain neutral.

The Autist Collective works with other Autists around the planet and even Autists from *other* planets. It is a group of "silent" and unsung heroes ushering in the New Earth and shedding light for humanity to witness, experience, and awaken to the truth about who and what humanity is.

Does Awakening the Autists Matter?

All Autists play a pivotal role in rebuilding our planet and bringing in the New Earth and the Divine Feminine energies. This information is underrepresented in written literature, yet its function is critical.

However, other groups, called by different names, are also working on bringing in the New Earth and Divine Feminine energies. Those other groups include the Lightworkers, Starseeds, Galactic Beings, Wayshowers, the 144,000, and New Children (Indigo, Crystal, Rainbow, Diamond, and Gold Children). These groups are connected; for example, some Lightworkers are Starseeds. The New Children are Starseeds. They all have roles.

You have a role in bringing in the New Earth also. We will get to that.

I've mentioned that not all Autists are awake or aware of their purpose or role. In their case, they will serve their function whether conscious of it or not—except, of course, it's all subject to free will.

Something that touched me so profoundly when I first met Lyrica Marquez and read her book was how she did not like her life before she awakened to her truth and remembered her role. She didn't care to be here. But this shifted when she awakened and remembered who she was and why she was here. Then, she loved her life, realizing she had a great purpose.

When you know your truth and live purposely, your life becomes filled with joy—the joy of purpose, fulfillment, and love for humanity. Energetically, when you're working on something you're meant to do, you're fueled by a greater power and experience the joy of being.

The Autists have their own awakening process. This was one of the reasons I wanted to write *The Unsuspected Heroes,* my visionary fiction novel that reveals the process Lyrica went through.

In the story, the Autist was the hero in the hero's journey, initially denying the call to adventure because she didn't know who she was. Then, she accepted the call. How? Her mother loved and honored her daughter unconditionally with her autism. In one distinct moment, the autistic character saw her truth and awakened, similar to Lyrica's experience.

Why is awakening the Autists important? Granted, they will do their work whether they know who they are and what their role is in this shift, but if you have an autistic loved one in your life, wouldn't you want them to love their life? Wouldn't you want to honor what they are doing for the planet? Wouldn't you like to thank them for their service?

Chapter 4:

AUTISTS: A CHANGING OF THE GUARDS

Just as humanity is evolving, so are the Autists.

ONE EVENING BEFORE A CHANNELING SESSION, Shauna Kalicki and I were at a restaurant waiting for our dinner, and suddenly Shauna mentioned, "Lyrica is here."

For the record, Lyrica was not physically with us at the restaurant. Shauna had psychically sensed her presence.

Lyrica Marquez is the first Autist I worked with. While at the table, Lyrica shared some personal information with Shauna in a clairaudient manner, and then she suggested that there would be a "changing of the guards" within the Autist Collective.

When Shauna went into a channeling session the next day, Cerian and Mother Mary came in. The first question I asked was about this "changing of the guards."

Cerian shared some personal information about both Lyrica and Daniel. Then they said, "Many young Autists are coming in at this point, bringing a different set of energies, more awakened and targeted energy that will be filling in and will be part of this collective network.

"There are node points or collective groups coming together across this planet. Much like the Christic grid, they have points of intensity, and to that sense, there is an additional or different type of work coming in. Know too that the Autistic Collective is also bound by their physical form and their ability to maneuver or hold specific energies.

"So, with this context, that comment from Lyrica is multifaceted. Some interesting new energies are coming in. Perhaps some of this collective are unable to work with, or work with as well as, the new Autist energetic beings that are coming in. The frequency they are coming in with or holding differs greatly from the Autists in the waves of awakening."

Our planet receives new energy all the time. The Autists work with these energies. In some ways, they are transformers and essentially transform the energies so humans can accept and work with the energy. Sometimes, the new energies are not new and have always been here, but humanity is being prepared and made ready to receive them.

The older Autists do not work with *all* the newer energies coming in. They work with specific energies they can "maneuver or hold," while the new Autists incarnating can handle some of these "newer energies."

Connie added that Daniel recently told her that the new Autists coming in are on a different level, and they can "smell and sense with their skin."

"We would use Dolores Cannon's terms, the first wave, the second wave, the third wave; they all had different purposes," Cerian continued. "This is also true of Autists. It is not that they are one and can work with, hold, and maintain all these energies. This is not true. Their physical form is bound by the laws of this particular planet. Their etheric form, their ability to maneuver in and out of certain specific frequencies, is what we would say is limited to their bodies' ability."

Cerian refers to the late Dolores Cannon, author of multiple books about the New Earth, one of which was *The Three Waves of Volunteers and the New Earth*. In that book, through hypnosis sessions, Cannon uncovered that three waves of beings volunteered to come to the planet to correct a "collision course with disaster."

Connie added, "This makes sense. When we were in Sedona, Arizona, Lyrica explained that Daniel and Leilah were more "advanced" than her as far as "flying through the realms" because they were younger than her. She brought a specific energy being born in the seventies. Leilah brought in a particular energy or wave born in the eighties, and Daniel brought a different wave in the nineties."

It is now the 2020s. "This makes sense that the newer generations bring in new energies," Connie concluded.

Daniel has indicated that more Autists are coming in because their work is needed in this evolution. He has also stated that Autists have their own evolutionary path. As new Autists come in to work with new energies, the older "waves" are going through their evolutionary process just as we are.

PART II

New Earth Back to Basics

Chapter 5:

WHAT EXACTLY IS THE NEW EARTH?

*We are currently experiencing a planetary shift
in consciousness. But if someone is unaware,
they won't be conscious of what is occurring.*

WE ARE IN A TIME OF SIGNIFICANT CHANGE, and some may suggest imminent evolution, but it is continuous and has been occurring for some time. The world you were born into is not the same world you are in today. The children born today are different from those of the earlier generation who are different from their parents.

This evolution will continue into a new age or era. One can liken it to an illumination, introspection, and even a Christic period. In my writing, I primarily use the term New Earth or New Earth energies because it broadly represents various beliefs, and I do not want to alienate readers. But it doesn't mean it is unique from some other concepts. The New Earth energies have been called by different names, such as the Divine Feminine, the Sophic, and Christic Grid energies, all of which are the New Earth energies.

What exactly is the New Earth? I want you to understand that there are many ways of saying what is happening on the planet. My guess is that you've heard some of them. Some people will say we are going through a consciousness shift. Others say paradigm shift or spiritual evolution, some call it ascension, and others refer to it as a planetary shift in consciousness. Several describe it as a dimensional shift from 3D to 5D, and I'm sure there are other phrases. All of these expressions are related.

But precisely what is it?

Humanity is evolving physically, spiritually, and energetically all at the same time. We are on an evolutionary path—a planetary shift in consciousness. This evolution has been in the making for ages. You can think of consciousness as intelligent awareness or perception of the inner and outer self. The inner "self" reflects the true self, emotions, feelings, thoughts, intuitions, hopes, dreams, and more.

At the same time, the outer "self" reflects what we offer the world about who we are. Are we presenting ourselves authentically or promoting facades? Let me ask you: are you being authentic? Are you showing the world who you genuinely are?

One way of looking at this evolutionary path is moving from consciousness to Consciousness (with an uppercase C).

Levels of Consciousness

Given that everything is energy, consciousness is also energy. It is energy that flows with intent or intelligence. Think of one's awareness as observing an action, while consciousness is the intelligence behind the action or observation. It is the state or quality or intelligence of awareness. It is what enables us to experience life as we know it.

From ancient civilizations to contemporary philosophy and psychology, humanity has studied consciousness. While there is no consensus among the many theories, many agree that there are different levels of consciousness.

Within the psychology arena, Freud suggested that several layers of awareness interact with each other to fashion the individual's personality and behaviors. He identified three "planes of awareness," which are levels of consciousness: the conscious mind, preconscious mind, and unconscious mind.

In the spiritual arena, one theory is that there are seven levels of consciousness; the first three levels are similar to Freud's planes of awareness:

1. **Waking consciousness** is where we live most of the time. You sense, feel, think, have memories, and make choices.
2. The **dreaming state** is what you experience when sleeping and dreaming. It can feel quite natural, though we sometimes have difficulty recalling our dreams.
3. In a **deep sleep**, one is unconscious and rests. You don't have an awareness of your experiences or memories and don't create new experiences.

Everyone should be able to relate to these first three levels as everyone experiences them. Four other levels of consciousness need development through energetic or spiritual practices, such as meditation, prayer, mindfulness, and contemplation.

1. In the **transcendental consciousness** level, you silence your senses (quiet your mind) while being conscious, which allows you to connect with your higher self without the influence of your thoughts, feelings, and memories.
2. In **cosmic consciousness**, you become aware of a world beyond you. Your everyday concerns begin to matter less. One may have fleeting moments of moving beyond to Oneness.

3. **God Consciousness** (or Oneness) is the level of deep connection with yourself and everything experienced in love, happiness, and discernment.

4. **Unity Consciousness** is the experience of One Consciousness. It is experiencing interconnectedness or no separation between yourself and everything.

These are levels of Human Consciousness. We are currently experiencing a *planetary* shift in consciousness. But if one is unaware, they won't be conscious of what is occurring. We are going from a dense, egoic state of consciousness, a state of separation from Source in the third dimension, to one that is a higher, lighter vibration of unconditional love in the fifth dimension. The 5D is a state of Unity Consciousness (in other words, Consciousness with a "Big C").

Think of the New Earth as your *experience of the shift in consciousness*. It is the experience of 5D or the experience of getting beyond the veil that obscures us from who we are. The New Earth is the experience of being harmonically in sync with Mother Gaia, who is conscious and fully alive. The New Earth experience is unique to each person and is already here, and the path to it is within.

Mother Gaia and Pure Autists Work in Tandem

There is a significant component in this shift that is often unspoken. Mother Gaia or Earth is alive. She is a living being. One reason our planet is in so much trouble today is that humanity has been in 3D consciousness, a state of separation, not realizing that we are *all* connected and all connected to Goddess Gaia.

Humanity has been unkind to Earth. It's a wonder Gaia hasn't flicked humanity off her like fleas through natural disasters because she certainly could. Instead, she has been patient. Why? Because she is aware of this *game* and has agreed to play. Yet, there is no doubt that there are other timelines, other parallel realities, where humanity pushes Gaia's buttons too many times, and our planet gets destroyed. In more than one channeling session, Cerian confirmed that Earth had a cataclysmic event in at least one timeline.

Mother Gaia and the Pure Autists are critical to the planetary shift. They both work in tandem. The Pure Autist energy, likened to Lemurian energy, must be anchored on Earth because humanity will miss the collective shift without it. Humanity does not have the momentum to shift without this energetic work. The Pure Autists have been part of the New Earth consciousness for many years. They bring both New Earth energy and New Planetary consciousness. Both these energies still need anchoring; this is why the autism rate has increased.

This is work that humanity cannot do because of the veil obscuring our memories. The Ethereal Autists have this memory, and many of the new Autists coming in have this memory. Very few of the Autists on this planet are from Earth. Does that make them aliens? Does that make them galactic beings? Cosmic beings? Starseeds? Yes.

Mother Gaia has one consciousness and one intelligence. She is evolving and moving into higher frequencies. She is ascending. Because of Gaia's vastness, her ascension will catalyze humanity's collective shift.

Mother Mary says that for the entire planet to shift, "All aspects of Earth must vibrate collectively. Otherwise, Earth cannot harmonically move into the vibrational pattern of the New Earth."

Those aspects of Earth that must vibrate together to make the shift are the various kingdoms, including rocks, minerals, plants, animals, water, and more.

Only a portion of humanity will make this shift as it is not every person's role to ascend to dimensions and experience the New Earth.

But every person has a role in the shift, and everyone must play it with the caveat that it is subject to free will and choice.

What are the roles? Be patient with me. Revealing each step slowly is important.

Chapter 6:

THE DIFFERENCE BETWEEN 3D, 4D, AND 5D CONSCIOUSNESS

We regularly shift in and out of 3D, 4D, and 5D experiences. The goal is to stabilize in 5D.

WE ARE EVOLVING from a lower egoic state to a higher, lighter form of Unity Consciousness, a state of unconditional love. We are shifting from 3D consciousness to 5D Consciousness. You may be wondering, what about 4D? Let's take this one dimension at a time.

What Is 3D Consciousness?

Third-dimensional consciousness is the state in which most experience life today. It vibrates at a frequency closer to fear, which is lower than the frequency of unconditional love. I've seen charts showing fear as low as 4 Hz to 100 Hz. In contrast, I've seen data showing unconditional love resonating from 400 Hz to over 800 Hz. Which is correct? Let's simply say that fear is a lower frequency than love.

The Ethereal Autist, Daniel, occasionally blogs on my website under "Daniel's Corner," and in one of his articles, he stated that all emotions are high frequency. This threw me because I typically suggest that fear is a low frequency, yet Daniel said, "Anything of God is high frequency."

So, it's relative.

In 3D, we experience life using our five senses and lead from our heads—our minds.

The third dimension is an egoic state of consciousness. We judge others by the clothes they wear, the cars they drive, their houses, and what they do for a living. We seek material items, social status, occupational standing, and money to satisfy us.

The third dimension is survival of the fittest, and people focus on the self, the individual, rather than the whole.

The third dimension has the experience of living in a duality of "good versus bad."

In 3D consciousness, we dismiss synchronicity as coincidence and serendipity as an accident. In truth, synchronicity and serendipity are miracles or messages from the Universe or Source—or what you may call God. Some even refer to them as Godwinks.

We believe our thoughts and words have no power and have no interest in turning inward to explore the deeper meaning of reality.

In 3D, we are human doings, not human beings. We are interested in *doing* rather than being. We fill our calendars to keep ourselves busy and boast about it. Then when facing a period of having nothing to do, we get bored, turn on the boob tube, and ignore an essential action—going inward.

Simply put, 3D is life in physicality but without a deep connection to Source Consciousness.

What Is 4D Consciousness?

Fourth-dimensional consciousness, or the 4D state, is a gateway or entrance to 5D Consciousness. In 4D, an individual uses the five senses along with some psychic abilities or intuition and their inner compass. My book, *Lifesigns,* is about working in 4D by recognizing these signs and tapping this inner guidance system.

Lifesigns are those messages from the Universe that guide us along our path. We all have them. The degree to which one pays attention to the "signs" will dictate how many messages one receives. These messages also include what I call the Universe's bricks, interference, unexplainable events, synchronicity, serendipity, or miracles.

Synchronicity and serendipity are different.

In 4D, we also understand a deeper meaning in signs, symbols, synchronicity, and serendipity.

Synchronicity is a meaningful coincidence orchestrated by the Universe to provide guidance, a message, or confirmation that one is on the right path. Serendipity is an event or situation that unfolds seemingly by accident or chance, resulting in unexpected good, something beneficial, or a favorable outcome.

Often, the two, synchronicity and serendipity, occur together. Both are a way of helping us improve our lives but, more importantly, awaken us to the truth that higher intelligence is guiding us toward something more significant: your Divine Blueprint and a New Earth.

Psychic abilities and intuition are different too.

In 4D, one may experience telepathy, clairvoyance, clairsentience, clairaudience, and other psychic skills, intuition, and dreams.

There is a considerable difference between psychic and intuitive hits, though the two are often confused. Think of a psychic message as sensing atypically with one of the five senses, while intuition is insight or inner knowing without having a reason to know it. It is learning from the higher self, the soul.

Know that you have these gifts. Everyone does. Again, the degree to which you pay attention to perceiving and receiving them with intention will determine your experience. The psychic gifts include the primary "clair" senses. Clair means *clear*.

- **Clairaudient** [clear hearing what is inaudible in the physical 3D realm]: Messages through words, thoughts, voices, music, or sound within our mind.

- **Clairvoyant** [clear seeing what is not in the physical 3D realm]: Visions, dreams, pictures, visual impressions, and auras seen from the third eye—the mind's eye. These can be sightings of alternate timelines (past, present, or future) and may be prophetic.

- **Clairsentient** [clear feeling what is not in the physical 3D realm]: Feeling energy and emotions connected to ourselves and others that may manifest as gut feelings, chills, empathy, physically sensing energy through warmth, tingling, or other experiences.

- **Clairalience** [clear smelling what is not in the physical 3D realm]: Smelling something when there is no odor source in physicality. Perhaps the scent of perfume, cigar smoke, chemical smell, or other smell when there is no apparent source.

- **Clairgustance** [clear tasting what is not in the physical 3D realm]: Tasting something without apparent reason or source of the perception.

- **Claircognizance** [clear thinking for no apparent reason]: Many refer to claircognizance as "clear knowing." Claircognizance can be those unexplained fleeting thoughts that come from nowhere and can be brilliant or even a warning. I call it "clear thinking," not to confuse it with intuition or epiphanies.

We do not process intuition through our filters.

Intuition, as I mentioned, is knowing from the soul, while psychic gifts are learning something through our senses. Psychic impressions go through the individual's personal and physical filters—their beliefs, values, attitudes, judgments, as well as one's physicality. The messages can be highly accurate if a person's filters are clean. Since intuition is from the higher self and not processed through filters, the information from intuition can be more reliable than psychic impressions.

In 4D, we are more empathic and compassionate toward others. We recognize that our thoughts and words have power. We start working with the law of attraction.

We seek out our purpose in life. In 4D consciousness, we treat our bodies better with exercise, diet, and practices, such as meditation or mindfulness. We seek to understand a deeper meaning to life and our purpose because we realize there is more than what we "see," and perhaps even the people we have chosen to follow misled us.

The fourth dimension is life in physicality with separation from Source (God), though we may ponder about or intellectually understand the concept of Oneness.

What Is 5D Consciousness?

Fifth-dimensional consciousness is living in unity consciousness, manifesting with a sense of Oneness with all hearts and souls of all beings and existence.

What is Oneness?

Oneness is the experience of being whole with the Universe, feeling connected with everything at every level. It is a state of being at one with Source, where there is no separation between the Self and

Source Energy. It is a state of re-membering—reassembling—with Source Consciousness. Oneness is the awareness that you are the observer and the observed.

Fifth-dimensional Consciousness vibrates at frequencies closer to unconditional love. We recognize there is no separation between ourselves and ALL; we see ourselves in others and Source. We realize we are all One, all equal, and wealth is not measured by the dollar. *Nothing needs measuring or judging.*

We are even more compassionate and empathetic than the 4D experience. In 5D, we lead with wisdom from the heart, not the head. In 5D, we recognize that we are creators and have unrestrained creativity. We live in unconditional love.

In 5D, there is no judgment. Things are not judged as "good" or "bad," as everything is an experience, and while duality will be a choice for life lessons in 5D, duality will not be at the level of 3D.

Cerian says, "The singular self [the individual] in 5D will be able to guide their will, choices, and creations more accurately and will express who and what they are naturally while in the fifth dimension."

In 5D Consciousness, we create our world quicker than in the lower dimensions. We live our Divine Blueprint authentically, our Truth as a sovereign being. Our experiences will be unique to each person.

We regularly shift in and out of dimensions. We may climb the dimensions from the third and fourth to the fifth and then fall back down to the third dimension because we haven't stabilized in the fifth dimension.

We may be having a great day experiencing being in the Universe's flow, then catch a crawler on a website revealing the stock market crashed. Perhaps at that moment, you wonder if you will have to continue working instead of retiring the following year. You go

43

to fear, your frequency plummets, and instead of being in 5D bliss, you're back to 3D fear.

"The New Earth is being experienced and shared by many now. You agreed to participate in this experience as a unified whole. Of course, you don't remember this, and that is the journey, one of awakening and remembering and claiming your sovereignty, which was hidden from humanity eons ago. Who hid it?

Fasten your seatbelt!"[2]

We will explore this further in the chapters to come.

Six Tips to Strengthen Your 5D Experience

Daniel shared some tips in *Destination New Earth* to help strengthen and stabilize in 5D. One was, "Experience life in a way that you don't seek anything. Be present and let life evolve naturally without forcing it."

Here are some suggestions from the earlier book to help move you into the fifth dimension and keep you there more and more.

- **Be aware** — Be available to know what is happening in your life. Learn safely through observation, awareness, and mindfulness. Examine everything. Our awareness is a catalyst to change and transform. Without awareness, we remain in the status quo. With awareness, we empower ourselves to evolve.
- **Be present** — There is only the now. Be fully conscious of the moment and free from the chatter of your inner

dialogue. Refrain from pondering events in your past or future. Eternity—timelessness—is in the moment and gained when appreciating what you have now with deep gratitude.

- **Be non-judging** — We are *not* here to judge the actions of others or ourselves. We are here to follow our hearts and live our Truth. Combatting judgment is part of this spiritual journey; the tools are compassion, empathy, love, and kindness.

- **Be curious** — Ask questions, and be curious about everything because the answers will take you places you haven't gone before. It will also help you understand emotions better. Curiosity awakens you to know yourself and your genuine relationship with Source. There is much power in asking questions.

- **Be open** — Being open is seeing things as they are and how they *could* make your life exciting. The truth is fluid. It changes as we grow. If we are so stubborn to refuse to consider actions, events, activities, matters, and so on, we will not evolve. *One cannot open their heart unless they are willing to consider new ideas.*

- **Be playful** — Exercise childlike enthusiasm, awe, and wonder when observing your world. By being playful, the burdens within diminish, and you open your mind and heart. When watching with awe and expectation, you see the magic, mystery, and miracles in everything, and life becomes joyful. You are here to experience. Why not enjoy it?[3]

Chapter 7:

STARSEEDS, NEW CHILDREN, AND GALACTIC BEINGS

"Do not forget that we are all hybrids,
and it was destined to be so."
—Daniel

WE LIVE IN A TIME OF EVOLUTION, and if you look at history, you may notice that revolution precedes evolution. That revolution and chaos have been occurring through natural disasters, wars, diseases, food crises, coronavirus, vaccines, and other catastrophes and will continue until the "old" Earth systems have collapsed. What will remain lasting will be those systems that support humanity as a collective, not as individuals.

This restructuring has occurred for some time, and some individuals play key roles in the revolution so humankind evolves. These people are called many names, including rebels, troublemakers, teachers, and healers, and countless groups have orchestrated this project of getting people to experience the New Earth throughout time. One group working knowingly or unknowingly is the New Children, who have come in various stages for decades.

STARSEEDS, NEW CHILDREN, AND GALACTIC BEINGS

The New Children Will Usher In the New Earth

Most Autists are Starseeds and New Children. They are assisting in bringing in the New Earth. The New Children have come in different groups, such as the Indigo Children, Crystal Children, Rainbow Children, Diamond Children, and Gold Children (and I'm sure there will be others).

All these New Children are Starseeds or Star People and play a role in humanity's spiritual evolution. Some refer to them as rebels, Wayshowers, "the 144,000," or Lightworkers. We may call them *children*, but many are now adults. They are here to usher in the change of humankind from its current state to a higher-dimensional being and the New Earth.

Starseeds Are from Other Worlds

If you believe that humanity is the only intelligent life-form in this universe, this will come as a shock. However, I don't think I will shock most who have chosen to read *Gods in the Game*.

Starseeds (Star Seeds) are beings incarnated in human form from other worlds; they are from other star systems. One may suggest that this is how aliens walk among us as humans. Others will say there are alien-human hybrids, which serves as an argument that aliens are among us. Except that humans *have* alien DNA, which is a better argument for "aliens walking among us." One could even suggest that since there is only the One, there is no such thing as an "alien." It doesn't matter where you hang your hat in this scenario because they're all true.

Some Starseeds may feel different, while others are clueless about being different. Their acceptance of themselves and the role they are to play depends on many factors: their generation, their family, friends, social standing, beliefs, and so forth.

For the newer generations coming in (Gold Children, Diamond Children, Rainbow Children, and Crystal Children), their acceptance of their roles will be easier than the Indigo Children, who are now adults, and the older generation of Starseeds who didn't get named.

Indigo Children or Indigo Adults are the rebels.

These individuals incarnated to bring about a new age of peace. Though not always, most were born throughout the late seventies to the early nineties. They are usually sensitive and psychic. Their role is to incite change in society, the environment, and government so that Earth is a place of integrity. They are often called the rebels, troublemakers, and even the *problem children* as they were growing up.

Crystal Children teach how to live from the heart.

The Crystal Children are second-generation New Children. These kids or adults started embodying in the mid-nineties and are still coming in. They are here to usher us into the New Earth by showing how people can live in kindness, peace, and love. They are full of integrity and often telepathic, though society may perceive them as slow or even autistic, and you know how I feel about autistic children, don't you? These individuals are far from slow. Living from the heart comes easily to them. They will teach us how to shift to the New Earth by living from the heart.

Rainbow Children are higher-dimensional beings.

The Rainbow Children are third-generation New Children. These children started coming in around the turn of the century and are still incarnating. They are higher-dimensional beings from perhaps the ninth dimension and convey pure love. As odd as this may sound, it is their first Earth incarnation, and they are here to generate *unconditional* love and will play an essential role in the New Earth as they age.

Many beings, such as the Rainbow Children and others coming to Earth for the first time, may have had imprints to prepare for their human experiences. One can think of an imprint as a download of various experiences or lifetimes of those who have lived on Earth. This way, the being has a memory of these experiences so that life on Earth is not so foreign to them. The concept of imprints explains why so many people may suggest that they have been, for example, the reincarnation of particular people, such as Cleopatra, Yeshua (Jesus), or Mary Magdalene, to name a few that seem to be "popular" reincarnations.

Another concept we will discuss later, split incarnations, parallel incarnations, or soul splits, also explains why some people may claim to share the same embodiment. In this case, their soul has more than one expression in the same timeline, and they each share perhaps a memory from their soul group.

Diamond Children are walking healers.

There are some Diamond Children here, though they are the exception to the rule. Diamond Children are fourth-generation Star Children, and as the Rainbow Children, some are first-timers to Earth. For these children to come in, adult Starseeds must spiritually evolve and birth the Diamond Child with a higher Light Quotient.

The Light Quotient determines the degree of Light one can hold in their energy field. Light is divine energy, and as it emanates and moves in all directions, it is one of the guiding factors in our soul expansion, not just our consciousness, and may sometimes be called Spirit.

Diamond Children possess the most advanced psychic skills,

including telepathic communication and telekinesis, and are instant manifesters.

Anger, hatred, fear, greed, and separation are as foreign to Diamond Children as Oneness is to most of the planet now. In other words, they are innately in the fifth dimension and beyond. The Diamond Child resonates with divine, pure, unconditional love.

They hold the DNA patterning that awakens all those near them who are ready to overcome the illusion. They are walking healers. However, the Earth's frequency must elevate to accommodate a significant mass of incarnating Diamond People. This is part of the Autists' work, striving to boost the frequencies.

Gold Children are energy conduits.

The newest wave or generation of New Children as of the writing of this book is the Gold Children. They began embodying in 2012, plus or minus a few years. According to Cerian, "They are powerful energy conduits and can help bring in and embody the new frequencies and harmonize the latest and the old frequencies or energies."

The new energies coming to the planet are New Earth energies. These energies have been here, though humans haven't been ready to receive them. The Gold Children hold specific energy that has been latent in Mother Earth and because of their presence, this energy is now awakening.

The Gold Children are "excellent transmitters" as they embody the new energies and harmonize them with the existing energies dormant within Mother Gaia, allowing for the bending of these two energies. According to Cerian, the Gold Children make it less challenging for Mother Earth and humanity to bring these energies in and work with them. These children receive and transform the New Earth energies so that the energies are easier for Mother Gaia and everything within and on Earth, including humans.

The Gold Children have an X-code (or Code X) in their DNA structure, which includes a new metallic substance, gold strands entwined in the DNA structure. This is why they are called the "Gold Children." That metallic substance is reminiscent of liquid gold, as it is soft and malleable and has Consciousness.

Cerian said, "It is the *unmanifest* expression that comes from the Creator. It moves into the manifest via the atom, proton, neutron, and electron, and operates like the cells within the human body."

It Begins with Code Carriers

A few years ago, I had a dream about a young boy. He was very friendly, and he was lying on his back. I leaned over, and when I looked into his eyes, they were gold with circuit boards, and I knew his name to be Austin. Through a series of synchronistic events in the days that followed the dream, I learned that there is an Ethereal Autist named Austin.

I've subsequently learned that Austin and three to four other children are X-code carriers on the planet. According to Cerian, these Code Carriers are "manifesting and holding these energies so that those coming in have a role model."

The Code Carriers hold this energy, Consciousness, and, by simply doing this, allow other Gold Children to do it, and they will wake up at an appropriate time. Cerian said, "Three to four children are like Austin and are markers and much like Daniel and his Collective. They are the outliers or the first, and then as they continue to hold the energy and work with it and live and be, it draws in more and more."

Cerian mentioned that the other three to four Code Carriers are not necessarily autistic, though Austin is.

As an amusing note, the transcript for this channeling, which mentions the Gold Children and Austin, was initially transcribed through an AI transcription service. Then, I read the transcript while listening to the recording, correcting the information where needed. I will say that oddly, three times in the transcription (twice during the Gold Children information and once following), the following appeared, which included a line break before and after the dialogues:

Hi.

There was no audible "Hi" in the recording—only silence. Cerian later confirmed that Austin was announcing his presence during the channeling.

Chapter 8:

SOME KEY DIFFERENCES ON WHAT'S BEING SAID

*No one path is correct. The best way for you is
the one that feels natural. Never follow another
so closely that you miss going inside.*

BEFORE WORKING WITH THE AUTISTS, I had read volumes of books on a wide variety of topics by many authors. I had a lifetime of curiosity and desire to seek out Truth that had encouraged my exploration of religion, spirituality, ancient civilizations, conspiracy theories, psychic phenomena, crystals, pyramids, myths, reincarnation, and many others.

When the Autists reached out to me, my reading interests expanded to learn about the New Earth. Then, after learning, I inquired with Mother Mary, Cerian, and Daniel about some of the material other subject matter experts and the Bible suggested.

I had an endless list of questions and still do. This chapter summarizes some differences between what our group learned versus the other experts. The humbling notion is that I realize how little I know the more I learn.

Some of this information is in *Destination New Earth,* and here, it serves as a refresher or a baseline to explore the concepts further.

You are the savior.

This evolutionary shift has been in the making for ages. Most of humanity has agreed to experience the change. Mother Mary, Daniel, and Cerian have all shared that it will probably happen, but it isn't a done deal, and humanity has work to do for it to come to fruition.

Mother Mary said, "The New Earth is formed, yet it is a probability and possibility, and humanity plays a large role in bringing it into humanity's awareness."

So, humanity has some work to do, and awakening is the work. One of the messages repeated in *Destination New Earth* is: wake up, realize who you are, play your role without judging others, and claim your sovereignty.

Perhaps it is from our religious upbringing or inherited behavior, as many expect a savior to save us. Many follow priests, ministers, philosophers, and spiritual leaders, hoping they will tell us what to do or where to expect the savior. *No savior is coming,* for each of *you* is the savior.

The New Earth is within you, and it is the self-realization that you are divine. Did I bury the lead? Yes, you are an expression of Source (God).

Not everyone will make it to the New Earth.

Some authors and spiritual leaders suggest that a significant event will occur, shifting everyone from the third to the fifth dimension. Essentially, everyone would "ascend." The information coming from our channelings did not see that happening. Instead, the shift will occur individually for quite some time. That means people will awaken around the planet until we reach a critical mass, and then a hundredth-monkey effect or tipping point will be reached, causing a greater awakening. But not all of humanity will make it to the New Earth, and that's okay because it's not everyone's role.

To simplify passages throughout this book, I may sometimes refer to the "Light Team" rather than repeatedly stating the various groups involved in this evolutionary shift. You can think of the Light Team as those here to assist humanity's awakening. Some people are here to awaken and help reach this critical mass to trigger a global awakening. Just as all humans have a unique blueprint and role in this shift, so do the Light Team members.

Light Team members have different roles in this shift.

There are numerous roles to play in this shift. Not all Light Team members are here to experience the New Earth. They may be here in positions of being a victim, an instigator, a healer, or even a villain. Light Team members' actions inspire others to awaken, which can happen with some people playing many different roles. For the Light Team member, their role won't always be the metaphoric lighthouse illuminating the way. Not all members of the Light Team are awake.

The point is that you never know the role an individual is playing. Only the individual can understand their soul's calling, their Divine Blueprint, and what role they are to play.

Everything is connected. You never know what inspiration a villain's horrendous act has on an emerging hero. The villain may serve a higher purpose in this shift, which is why the message of being nonjudgmental is essential.

There are more experiences available in 3D than in 5D.

I've read about the speculations that there will be a split of Earth, forming two planets, one Earth remaining in the third dimension and one ascending to the fifth dimension. Others suggest that the 3D

Earth will end in an apocalypse while those going to 5D Earth will ascend to the heavens. However, this is not what our work revealed.

The information from our channelings suggested that those remaining in 3D, those not shifting, will still have the same trials and tribulations as they usually have. Life for these people may not be easy for them. The experience of remaining in 3D is their choice. It is part of their journey and the lessons they have chosen.

The lower the dimension one encounters, the more there is to experience. More experiences are available in 3D than in 5D. We should not judge a person's decision to remain in 3D, which has more duality and opportunities for powerful spiritual lessons.

Many remaining in the 3D may resent that life is easier for those shifting to higher dimensions. Those accessing and stabilizing in the 5D will be more in the flow of the Universe and experience more ease and grace.

When I say "the Universe," I refer to what you may call God, Spirit, Source, the I AM, Higher Intelligence, Consciousness, or whatever you call your highest ideal.

There will be a separation between people.
We did not see a split forming two planets. There will be one Earth, and the people experiencing different dimensions will coexist on the planet together.

There will be a separation between the two peoples, those desiring to evolve energetically and those not. While this separation is a choice because we always have free will, it has been occurring. We are drawn to people of like energy naturally. Perhaps you have seen some separation from people in your own lives. Perhaps longtime friends, family members, and significant others are phasing out of your life.

This separation between yourself and loved ones is a natural occurrence and a choice.

There will be New Earth communities.

People are drawn to like energies and will disperse into groups and communities of like minds. There will be an emergence of smaller, self-sustaining communities where people with fifth-dimensional ideals will migrate. These communities will have simpler lives. Their values will reflect supporting the community as a whole family rather than the individual. They will share responsibilities, not for monetary gain because they recognize the macrocosm. Each will see their contributions serving the whole, not the individual.

As people awaken, these communities will thrive, creating their New Earth collectively, not individually. Their manifestations will be more instantaneous, and their creations will be magnificent. And therefore, the communities will be glorious.

The New Earth is a hologram.

There is a theory called holographic duality. Think of 3D as having three reference points (e.g., a cube has height, length, and width) while 2D (second dimension) has only two references (e.g., a map has width and height). Holographic duality suggests that the 3D Universe is mathematically strung to a 2D universe. The theory suggests that a 3D hologram projects by a 2D complex system of interconnected elements, or web.

If we apply this theory to our existing world, it would be a hologram, and the New Earth is also a hologram.

The New Earth is within you.

The New Earth is already here—*but we are looking for it in the wrong direction.*

Humanity is looking for someone to save us, which may be our ancestors' genetic inheritance of behavior. When humankind was first created, we wanted a leader to follow. We wanted instructions on survival, so we followed our leaders mindlessly, relinquishing control to a select group. We surrendered our sovereignty and became controlled.

Today, people still follow the establishment. They admire politicians, corporate leaders, teachers, athletes, musicians, doctors, actors, spiritual leaders, and religious leaders. We continue to look outside ourselves for leaders to enlighten us on the New Earth.

There is fifth-dimensional energy in humanity's subconscious now. The New Earth is here, and humanity subconsciously is expecting it. However, we are watching for it but looking for it in the wrong direction. The people you follow *will not* be able to show you the New Earth, for the New Earth is to be found within each of us.

There are outstanding teachers, spiritual leaders, and role models we have followed; perhaps they have taught us the tools to grow. Yet, do not follow anyone so closely that you miss going inside. It is time to take the tools we've learned from them and, assuming they feel pure and direct us inward, use them.

There is no one correct tool or process to get you there. Every path is unique. The way for you is the one that feels natural, where you can surrender and permit your higher self to lead the way.

I've mentioned that we are expecting this shift. Most of us agreed to experience it. We consented to partake in the occurring chaos, which will continue until the shadows are exposed and resolved. It is all part of the game, which has been in the making since Lemuria.

Humanity will have some difficult times ahead. Many of these are "tough love" situations that expose the shadows and Controllers so humanity will awaken. Again, how we navigate the chaos will help humanity get through the revolutionary part of the shift.

Chapter 9:
YOUR DIVINE BLUEPRINT

*When our choices align with our Divine
Blueprint, our lives are more abundant, joyful,
fulfilling, and flow easily and gracefully.*

ONE CAN THINK OF A DIVINE BLUEPRINT as a detailed description of your divine plan and life purpose set before incarnating. It contains the design for your soul's destiny or ultimate life path. It goes beyond what you may call your "purpose in life" yet includes it. It is a design of staying aligned with your soul and a template or guide to what you are to do in this lifetime. It *is* the expression of your higher self in physicality.

Keep in mind that we all have free will and free choice. It isn't that we are stuck on a path to fulfill our Divine Blueprint—we are put on a path, and what we do with it is up to us. If we head toward the blueprint, the Universe, Source, God will respond differently than if we run away from it. In the latter case, one may feel events as if fate intervened.

When asking Cerian to give a simple definition for Divine Blueprint, they said, "The simplest term is to be your Self."

I capitalize Self here to indicate your higher self or your soul.

Cerian continues, "The Divine Blueprint resides within, and if you just listen—not with your ears, but with your heart—it is what you most desire. Or it could be a calling or a longing. It is who you are, and it is to express that, and when we mean 'express,' we mean to live it—to be it, to already know you are it."

The Divine Blueprint is to live your Soul's Truth. Be who you are destined to be. Be your higher self.

Cerian shared that as a human being, you are always sacred. Before you incarnated, you wrote a contract to come to Earth to experience, and within you, in your high heart, you have the wisdom to live that Divine Blueprint. I like to think of the high heart as a gateway within us to connect with our higher self.

"We would always say that it is pure intent of growing, expanding, being yourself. So, its simplicity is just to *be—to be yourself* [your Self]. That is your Divine Blueprint."

Each person's blueprint is unique, though some may have similarities with other individuals. When living your blueprint, you live authentically. In other words, the Divine Blueprint is the authentic self. When you live authentically, the events of your life are in the flow.

Each person has a unique role in this shift in consciousness. Like your soul's purpose, your role in this spiritual evolution is within your soul's design. What your part is *only you know*. It is not a question to ask your favorite psychic, life coach, or minister. Your higher self has the answer.

The Universe, Source, Consciousness guides you along the way. Your life responds to whether you live your Divine Blueprint or not.

We create our lives through thoughts, feelings, emotions, and decisions. When our choices align with our Divine Blueprint, our lives are more abundant, joyful, fulfilling, and flow easily and gracefully.

Whereas, if our decisions don't align with the soul, we won't be content. We may feel stuck or stagnant. We may even find the Universe sending bricks occasionally to get us back on course. As mentioned, this may feel a bit like fate interrupting our lives.

Some bricks put you back on course.

I have always been driven to seek and fulfill my soul's purpose. In the early nineties, I began my spiritual journey after going through a turbulent time, with a miscarriage, being attacked because of my sexual orientation, and multiple litigations. These "bricks in life" stirred me to ask all *those* questions: Who am I? Why am I here? What is my purpose in life?

My quest led me to attend a spiritual retreat on finding my purpose. This retreat was indeed stepping outside the box because, up until then, I would have considered myself strictly religious, and I was a scientist by education and training. I hadn't explored metaphysics at all.

After the weeklong event of playing with both left-brain and right-brain exercises, I walked away with a mission statement to be a catalyst for change and help people respect individual differences. One oddity that came through that week was that I was to use writing as a tool to serve my purpose. This surprised me as I wasn't a writer; indeed, it was one area I did not excel in. And yet, a decade earlier, a fleeting thought crossed my mind: *If I ever write a book, its title will be* Facades.

By the end of the conference, energetically, I was fueled with purpose. Before I left, I got a call from my lawyer—the turbulence in my life began stabilizing. And a month later, I was pregnant. While pregnant, my creativity blossomed, and an idea for a book came to me that aligned with my purpose. And the title, *Facades,* fits the story. *Facades* was my first book, published in 2000.

This period was joyful for me—a time of ease and grace. I learned how the Universe responds when living purposefully and living my truth. I also learned that the Universe guides us through gentle suggestions, but they become bricks or feel like fate when we fail to see and respond to them.

Your soul has a unique sound.

Something else happens when you live your truth; your inner or true self matches your outer self. When I say "true self," I mean your emotions, feelings, thoughts, intuitions, hopes, and dreams. When I say "outer self," I mean what you present to the world about who you are. Are you showing the world who you genuinely are?

Each soul has a unique harmonic resonance frequency: a note or a sound. When we live our Truth—when that true inner self matches that outer self, we live authentically, play our soul's note or frequency, and affect everyone. That makes *you* important to this planetary shift in consciousness.

The best gift you can give yourself and the world is to live authentically with sovereignty, live your Truth, and see the Truth of others while remaining nonjudgmental as you permit them to have their own consciousness. By living your Divine Blueprint, you provide a gift to the world.

What's in your spiritual toolkit?

Gods in the Game is not a beginner's spirituality book. You are on a spiritual path, but the way can be lengthy, and everyone is at a different point. You likely have adopted spiritual principles and practices and regularly apply them. For those who haven't, I list some of my methods here. That doesn't make them correct for you, though; I offer them here only if they feel natural.

1. **Journal** — I suggest getting one if you do not have a journal. Journal daily and monitor how your inner world creates the outer world—because that is what happens; it's not the other way around. You are the creator of your world and the scientist too. Monitor how the Universe reacts to your changes. When changing anything, note it and record how your world responds.

2. **Meditate** — If you do not meditate, begin. Even five minutes a day helps. Find a time each day that you can commit to. Create your sacred space and build your altar. Bring in the elements: earth (a plant, crystal, sage), wind (the breath), fire (a candle), and water (a fountain or glass of water). A chair or mat—it doesn't have to be fancy. It doesn't have to be sitting or lying. It can be a meditative walk or hike. The objective is *not* to have a remarkable experience (such as a vision, out-of-body experience, past life memories, and the like). The goal is to clear your mind and reach a state of inner peace.

3. **Thoughts become things** — We may study the law of attraction, but do you apply it? If you do not monitor your thoughts and spoken words and live by the concept, thoughts become things, consider beginning now. Your spoken words and thoughts are instructions you give to the Universe, and you are powerful. Please keep your thoughts and words positive, as, on the one hand, they are the seeds we plant. On the other hand, they can hurt others. According to Daniel, "Thoughts are like razors," as some people, like Autists who are highly sensitive to energy, can actually "feel" them.

4. **Clean your temple** — In this shift, you prepare to integrate your higher self into physicality. Your body is the temple. When you invite guests over, do you clean your house?

Understand that what you surround yourself with, what you consume as food and drink, what you hear, what you watch, how you feel, what you contemplate, and what you express changes your frequency. Is your body moving and well-exercised? Do you spend time in nature? All these actions impact your frequency, and at this time, you need to raise it. You don't have to be a purist, but you do need to make your temple inviting for the ultimate guest—your higher self.

5. **Live your life as if everything is a miracle** — By embracing the awe and wonder of life and expressing gratitude for everything, significance appears in the smallest details. There is a snowball effect here. It begins with a molehill and surpasses the majesty of a mountain. Remember that you attract like, so if you approach life in gratitude, what you are grateful for will manifest. If you're happy, happy people will come to you. If you marvel at the ordinary, the extraordinary emerges.

These are some practices I have in my toolkit. Perhaps you have others. The thing about tools is that they are *only* helpful when used. Try them daily and see if you perceive a shift in frequency.

Exercise — Are you on course to achieve your Divine Blueprint?

As mentioned, only you can determine your Divine Blueprint. For those who are not sure, I've included this exercise to help gauge whether you are on the right path.

Think of your Divine Blueprint as true north on a compass. When heading toward your blueprint (north), your life should flow easily, gracefully, and joyfully with great fulfillment. If this is your experience, this is a good indication that you are heading in the right direction or living your blueprint.

If this is your situation, honor that, and if you change something in your life and suddenly receive a shift in energy through some difficulty, stagnation, or disruption, consider the possibility that you have deviated from "true north"—your Divine Blueprint. Or, consider the possibility that the change is simply not for your highest and best good. In either case, it may be a gentle nudge from the Universe. And it is your choice whether to return to the status quo or continue the change.

If your life is generally not easy and grace-filled, if there is routinely a sense of fated interference from the Universe, like no matter what you do, it's as if you're driving with the brakes on, then take it as a sign that you are off course. The degree to which you are astray may depend on whether the Universe sends gentle nudges to get your attention or slams you with bricks to wake you up.

This would be an excellent time to pull out your spiritual toolkit, especially your journal, and see if working on the principles provides some relief.

Additionally, think about when the Universe's signs began. What has put you off course from your ultimate path? If it's obvious, e.g., life just started getting difficult after starting a new job, developing a new relationship, a new habit, a new friend, a recent move, or some other change, consider the possibility that the change is not heading toward your Divine Blueprint.

If this is your situation and it's obvious, try to change it and see how the Universe responds. If you suspect but are not entirely convinced, try an incremental change. In either case, journal the changes you're making and how your life responds to them.

Give it time, patience, and practice daily. Change one aspect of your life at a time and see what happens. Remember, you are the scientist and creator of your world.

Shauna's Five Journaling Tips

Here are some of Shauna's journaling tips:

1. Ensure you have easy access to your journal throughout your day.
2. As you become aware of your thoughts, feelings, decisions, intuitive knowing, and signs from the Universe, such as synchronicity, serendipity, psychic hits, and unexplained events, jot them down quickly in a few words.
3. Pick a quiet time each evening to dive deeper by reviewing your notes throughout the day and reflecting on what occurred.
4. If anything noteworthy happened, with pen in hand, consider fleshing out the event and exploring it in more depth:
   a. Where were you?
   b. How did you feel?
   c. What were you doing?
   d. Was anyone with you?
5. In the days to follow, identify patterns or themes occurring in your life. Is it a pattern you want to change? If so, what do you need to do to change it?

There are volumes of books written on spiritual practices that may help. If you want to learn more about how the Universe guides you through everyday life events and add to your spiritual toolkit, consider reading *Lifesigns: Tapping the Power of Synchronicity, Serendipity and Miracles.*

Chapter 10:

HUMANS ARE
MULTIDIMENSIONAL BEINGS

*Treat others the way you like to be treated—because
you never know when you will meet your "self."*

SOME SAY HUMANS are multidimensional beings. If we are experiencing 3D, 4D, and 5D, this undoubtedly means we are multidimensional. However, there is another level of multidimensionality that warrants further exploration.

What is a multidimensional being?

Multidimensional beings have other incarnations, other lives, or other expressions of themselves in different dimensions and in different timelines at the same time. The simultaneous lives are considered various expressions of a soul.

A human being is a physical expression of a soul, but the soul simultaneously has multiple expressions throughout time and space. The soul has different lifetimes that we may perceive as being in the past, future, and current timeline.

These soul expressions can be human, alien, angelic, elemental, animal, organic artificial intelligence (AI), consciousness, or other matter. Yes, I said AI. For this discussion, organic artificial intelligence is a person without a divine Spark of Life (aspect of the soul). They are not on the same evolutionary path as humans, but they are here to experience on behalf of a soul or Oversoul. The concept of organic AI or backfill people is explored further in *Destination New Earth: A Blueprint to 5D Consciousness*.

The Spark of Life is an aspect of a soul.

A human is an expression of a soul, and the soul is also called the higher self. A Spark of Life is a part of the soul and is contained within the human, but not in the *physical* body.

According to yogic and Vedantic beliefs, humans have physical, causal, and astral bodies. The soul's Spark of Life is within the causal body, and the causal body is within both the physical and astral bodies.

The Spark of Life is what makes a human being Divine.

Think of the soul group as an octopus.

For simplification purposes, I think of the soul, or soul group, depicted as an octopus.

I say "soul group" because the soul has multiple expressions or lifetimes that may be considered past or future lifetimes. These expressions form the soul group.

We often think of these expressions of our soul group as past lives. However, the term "past lives" is incorrect for different reasons. First, all lifetimes occur concurrently so there are no past or future lives. But also, each "self" is unique to the soul group. When the "self" dies or transitions, its experiences are absorbed by the soul. While there may be a memory of those experiences among the "soul group," the "self" does not return in another lifetime.

Multidimensionality of the Soul

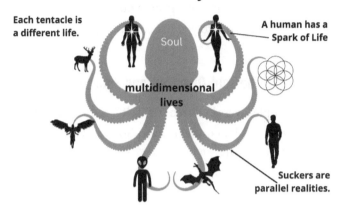

Each expression, each lifetime, is unique. Depending on the individual's blueprint, the "self" may have memories of these other lifetimes of the soul group and interpret them as "past life" memories.

You may think of the head of the octopus as where other multidimensional expressions, other lifetimes, connect. Each tentacle represents a different life or expression. Each tentacle has countless suction cups, or suckers, symbolizing our parallel realities. This metaphor illustrates how humans are multidimensional at the soul level or soul group, not at the Spark of Life, as it is an aspect of the soul.

When one integrates their higher self, their soul, within their physicality, depending on the person's Divine Blueprint, one *may* fully recall the other expressions of their soul group or have access to their gifts *if* it is within the individual's blueprint. More importantly, in the awakening, you are a co-creator, and you do not need the gifts of your soul's other expressions, for you will have access to everything.

These tentacles or lifetimes are so close together and often entwined with each other. The other lifetimes can impact each other, and your life—the "self"—can affect other soul expressions. Depending on your Divine Blueprint, you may even have another soul expression reach out to you to communicate with you.

The Soul, Oversoul, and Source

There are multiple layers between the "self" and Source. Humanity cannot understand its connection to Source, God. Daniel, the Ethereal Autist, suggests, "Think of it all as ONE."

Consider for a moment that there is one soul, the Oversoul. The Oversoul is the unity of all souls that transcends all individual consciousnesses.

"While we have this insistent need to understand and put things in some hierarchy, consider that from the self to Source is one energy, and all its levels combined are one and whole, and that is Oneness."[4]

I offer Daniel's words when I try to understand concepts beyond my grasp, "Keep the curiosity and let go of the need to know."

Energetic Beings Having a Human Experience

You have a Divine Spark of your soul within, and as previously indicated, when a human transitions, the Spark of Life returns to the soul.

You are a spiritual or energetic being having a physical or human experience. At the soul level, you are not physical; one could even suggest that physicality is an illusion.

Your soul, which is not you, has multiple experiences simultaneously in other realms or dimensions. Some of these experiences are physical, and others are unworldly, spiritual, consciousness, or in the ethereal realms.

Golden Rule: Treat Others the Way You Like to Be Treated

Your soul may even have different expressions, different lives, on Earth simultaneously. Some refer to this as split incarnations, parallel incarnations, or soul splits, not to be confused with a twin soul. In the latter case, the masculine and feminine division creates two souls with unique experiences.

"What does all this mean? It is possible, yet not probable, to meet another expression of your soul. Perhaps this knowledge sheds some light on the Golden Rule: *treat others the way you like to be treated* (because you never know when you'll meet your "self")."[4]

PART III

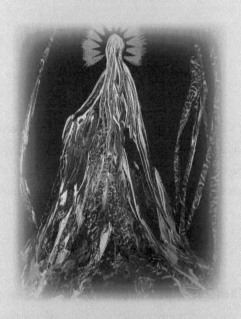

Awakening

Chapter 11 :

WHAT IS SPIRITUAL AWAKENING?

*"In the awakening, you are the co-creator. You don't
need to access anything other than your current
higher self. There is nothing that you cannot do,
perceive, or access—as you are already complete."*
—Cerian

AN AWAKENING IS A NEWFOUND AWARENESS of an energetic
reality. We undergo many awakenings in a lifetime, and certainly
during this evolutionary shift in consciousness, because there are
many types of awakening.

Awakening is an individual's personal experience and is unique
to each person. It can occur slowly over a long period while a person
is on the spiritual path or spontaneously. While we may strive for
the ultimate awakening, often called enlightenment, there are other
types of awakening worthy of mention, and they do not necessarily
occur in a specific order.

Before diving into the different types, I want to share an awakening, though I'm not sure if I'd call it a spontaneous soul awakening

or a mind awakening. Perhaps it was a bit of both because it changed how I view my world. The following occurred in the early 1990s.

An Out-of-Body Experience to Share

I was in bed, asleep, beside my partner. I was dreaming . . . or at least I thought so. I floated out of my body toward the ceiling. I could see my body lying in bed with my partner. I was ethereal, holographic-like, and aware that I was in two places simultaneously. This awareness made me wonder if I was having a lucid dream, one of those dreams you have when you're aware you're dreaming.

At the time, I was skeptical of anything one would call woo-woo, occurrences one perceives as "out there." I had a fleeting thought: *This is an out-of-body experience.* But my disbelief in anything supernatural quickly dismissed it.

My body floated away from the bed toward the open French doors leading to a balcony. I peered over the railing and glimpsed the Christmas lights illuminating the top of the fireplace and the closet near the front foyer below. I inched over the balcony above the open area, wondering if I'd fall. Still, before finishing the thought, I slowly and gracefully floated down to the front foyer until I was by the front door.

I stared at the door's deadbolt, and my skeptical side emerged. I plotted to leave the house with the door unlocked to see if the deadbolt remained unlatched in the morning. Interestingly, as I planned to test if this was happening, the thoughts seemed to coincide with my actions. I went outside and closed the unlocked door. In no time, I was out the door facing Denver's lights from my elevated location in the foothills. I turned away from the lights and headed into the mountains.

In the morning, when I woke, I sat up so fast it jarred my partner awake. She asked if everything was okay, and I told her about my odd dream and how I left my body and went out the front door and left it unlocked to see if it happened.

Without saying anything, she left the bedroom and went downstairs. She returned a few minutes later, crawled beneath the comforter, and lay quietly. When I asked if something was wrong, she said, "The front door was unlocked."

I started looking at life differently after this. I could no longer say things were woo-woo and roll my eyes, which I was very good at, I might add.

This experience, indeed, was an awakening.

Energetic Awakening or Kundalini Awakening

An energetic awakening is when a shift or intensification occurs in the body and energy system, affecting how the person experiences themselves and the world. Energetic openings often dramatically open someone to new levels of consciousness, embodiment, and the intensity of their energy.

Various ancient practices call this energy qi, prana, or kundalini. Qi gong, tai chi, yoga, meditation, and tantra can help awaken this energy. However, one can have a spontaneous kundalini awakening.

Physical signs of an energy awakening can include energy rushes, tingling, feelings of electrical pulses, change in libido, a more profound awareness of intuition, and interconnectedness. There can be a deep sense of purpose and an impulse to make life changes.

It can also be uncomfortable and promote fear if the individual does not know what's occurring. In such cases, one can experience appetite changes, hypersensitivity, insomnia, or highly altered states of consciousness, to name a few.

This energetic opening may be temporary or permanent and can open a person to a new awareness or embodiment. Embodiment is the infusion of more Light from the higher self, the soul, into physicality.

In the late nineties, I was introduced to meditation when I began working on my psychic development. While at a weeklong conference, we meditated daily. I quickly realized I was clairsentient as I could feel the energy. This was indeed an awakening for me. It shocked me to feel my own skin tingling and vibrating. While it is difficult to describe, this sensation still occurs today when I meditate, do Qi gong, or simply get quiet inside.

Mind Awakening Can Be an Aha Moment

A mind awakening is mentally realizing something new about the world intellectually. It can be the experience of an aha moment, an intuitive leap, an epiphany. Also, it could be suddenly seeing synchronicity, serendipity, or other signs as being meaningful. Perhaps a piece of information clicks into place to broaden, deepen, and enrich one's understanding of life. Another example would be awakening to the realization that everything is energy and you are an energetic being.

At one point in my life, it hit me that the Universe sent me messages with synchronicities and serendipities. It was an intellectual observation that led me to use more of my intuition. I understood that every person is intuitive and has psychic gifts. This awakening changed how I navigate life. It became a creative source for earlier novels and inspired my book *Lifesigns*.

Personality Awakening Ignites a New Path

A new personality awakening is when a substantial shift in one's behaviors, thoughts, and emotions occurs. The change results from attaining a deeper connection with oneself, perhaps identifying and eliminating patterns that do not serve while developing practices that do. One may find a new path in life more aligned with one's soul and live more authentically.

At some point, I wanted to be a successful writer with a platform and ample following and support myself through writing. I prayed on this. Today, I am a successful writer and support myself through writing, but not my books. However, that is changing, and I write this with a smile.

Perhaps I wasn't clear when working on manifesting my dream, yet I believe it worked out better. I not only write books, but I also write for clients. It hit me that I am helping my clients live their dreams by writing for them. It isn't necessarily work that inspires my soul, but writing that is important to my clients, and I can see their businesses thrive. Seeing my clients' dreams come true and knowing that my work contributes to their growth is incredibly satisfying.

More importantly, today, I realize that if I had continued a more public lifestyle, I would not be as happy as I am. I do not think I would be living authentically. I am better at maintaining a lifestyle of solitude, peace, and creativity.

Soul Awakening Is a Deepening with Your Higher Self

A soul awakening can occur suddenly or over a long period. It can also be brief, fleeting, or long, permitting one to look at enlightenment and see one's Truth. That Truth is that you are divine, an expression of Source energy.

When long-term soul awakening occurs, contact with the higher self deepens. The higher self is the soul. One may unite with their soul purpose, live their Divine Blueprint, and connect with their soul aspects from other lifetimes and spirit guides. Significant consciousness expansion can exist to embrace the cosmos. There may be an opening to a deeper connection to Source.

In a soul awakening, one may experience moments where there is no separation between oneself and Source. As this happens, insights permeate into awareness, and one may increasingly identify authentically as an evolving soul.

"The Octopus is a good example of the soul." —Mother Mary
Mother Mary has guided the direction of this book from a bridge book to expanding the concepts of *Destination New Earth*. Within that book, we talked a bit about multidimensionality. I later came up with using the idea of an octopus to describe the soul and soul group, as shared in the previous chapter.

While engaged in a channeling session for this book, Mother Mary said, "The octopus was a good example" of the soul and soul group. At the time, it amused me that she was aware of my metaphor because it had never been a topic in our discussions.

Recently, I participated in an ancient ceremony of consuming psilocybin mushrooms with a traditional cacao drink. Both medicines have been used for religious and spiritual purposes for thousands of years. This was my first experience, and I did this with a small group and wasn't exactly sure what to expect. Before the ceremony, I was guided to be clear about my intentions, and I worked on refining them for nearly a month before the journey. One of my primary intentions was to connect with my higher self or soul and soul group. Another intention was to experience Source.

The medicine "hit" me about an hour into the experience. My third eye woke, and when I closed my eyes, I was startled to see red tentacles with suction cups intertwined and moving. *An octopus?* I wish I could say I engaged with it more, but its movement made me nauseous, so I had to come out. This vision occurred multiple times during the experience.

The vision confirmed how I thought of the soul and the soul group, but I also became aware of how close and intertwined these other lifetimes are and how they impact each other.

The next substantial realization was: *This medicine is not my path to God.*

The term "God" surprised me as I typically use "Source" or the "Universe." I beat myself up for some time as I had consumed the medicine and knew it wasn't my path. Then I heard, *Everything in life is for the experience*, reverberating in my head. I was encouraged not to waste this experience.

The experience evolved, and with it came an awareness that I was both the Observer and the observed. I was the Creator and the creation. This awareness came while I meditated on a hill with a swirling, frigid wind around me.

When I opened my eyes, I recognized I was both the death in the dormant vegetation and the life in the sprouting early spring grass. I was the mountain rising before me and the water in the lake behind me. I was the sky, the clouds, the sound of the wind, and the wind itself.

What made the experience remarkable to me was that when I focused on an item, what lay in front and behind blurred and shrunk. But the object of focus grew in vibrant color, size, and dimensionality—with magnificent colors I hadn't seen before.

In my experience, I was aware I was the New Earth—and what a great confirmation of the adage, "What we focus on grows."

Today, I know that medicine permitted me to see beyond the veil. When I had the awareness that I was the New Earth, it was that I had the Unity Consciousness experience. The New Earth is the experience of the fifth dimension.

I've always known that what we pay attention to grows, but this was growth in a new and exciting way. I had known that the New Earth is within each of us but hadn't quite put it in the perspective that each of us is responsible for creating and building our New Earth.

I know *that* medicine is not my path. I also know that it gave me an experience of seeing beyond the veil, which was a gift, and I look forward to experiencing that again, but not under the influence of medicine.

Awakening to the Truth or Enlightenment

Some refer to the ultimate spiritual awakening as enlightenment, self-realization, nirvana, or *awakening to the Truth about who you are*. In this type of awakening, the person penetrates the veil that shields one from the Truth that they are not separate from Source. The individual moves into a higher level of Consciousness and a higher, lighter vibrational frequency—shifting from the denser, egoic state of duality consciousness to Unity and heart-based Consciousness.

In this case, there is a collapse between experiencing as the individual and the All—One. Here, the self dissolves, and what remains is Unity. It is the experience of Oneness. This rare experience can occur spontaneously or after years of spiritual discipline. It is a gift of grace, a mystical awakening that transcends the mind.

Cerian offers, "In the awakening, you are the co-creator. There is nothing you cannot do, perceive, or access."

You do not need to access your past or future lifetimes because you are complete and whole.

"You don't need to access anything other than your current higher self," Cerian said.

Do not *try* to awaken.

Cerian said, "Just do. The awareness of the faith of the mustard seed is truly what it is. Humanity does not have faith that they can do it."

For those unfamiliar with the biblical reference, *"For truly I tell you, if you have faith the size of a mustard seed, you will say to this mountain, 'Move from here to there,' and it will move"* (Matthew 17:20-21 (KJV)).

Cerian continued to say that without faith, one won't awaken.

Faith is a deep inner knowing that what you seek is already yours for the taking. It is the assurance of things you hope for.

Some speculate the center of faith is the pineal gland in the middle of the brain, and when concentrating on this area, one opens to spiritual faith.

Developing faith is essential to spiritual realization. Faith is more powerful than belief, and we know the power of belief. When working in spiritual substance and creative law, faith accomplishes all things. When faith is exercised deep in spiritual consciousness, it brings miracles.

Chapter 12:

A HIGHER LEVEL OF AWAKENING

*"When humans recognize that they are a
conduit of energy, an expression of energy, they
can consciously work with this energy."*
—Cerian

WHILE TALKING WITH CERIAN through the psychic medium Shauna Kalicki, I read the following passage to Cerian, which sparked an interesting conversation between us.

"In *Destination New Earth*, we reveal: 'The shift will occur individually, meaning one person at a time until the planet reaches a critical mass that will trigger a significant portion of humanity to ascend. At *that* time, those humans on an evolutionary path will ascend to the fifth dimension.'"[5]

"To me," I continued, "this suggests that we need more and more people to awaken or shift until we reach a certain percentage of the population. Then there'd be a more significant awakening on the planet. There are various types of awakening, including mind awakening, energy awakening, soul awakening, and enlightenment.

"When Cerian suggest that there has to be a 'higher level of awakening,' what type of awakening must that be?" I asked.

"We were thinking about this as you asked that question," Cerian admitted. "It doesn't have to be a specific number of people. It is not the individuals. It's the awakening or the consciousness within individuals and those varying levels. The critical mass [that needs to be reached] is the awareness of humanity being energetic beings."

At this point, Cerian cautioned about using the term "spiritual" too much within the book, as "spiritual" can be a trigger word for some readers, suggesting religion or Spirit. For this reason, I do my best to use the term "energetic" throughout this text.

Cerian stopped speaking at this point. The channel, Shauna, quieted for a bit. Then they began again.

"So, as we are playing with this," Cerian explained, "we too are getting a download coming through that we want to share through the channel, and that is, again, it's a very simplistic term—energy."

We Are Energetic Conduits

"Energy cannot be created nor destroyed, but it can be transformed," Cerian began. "When humans recognize that they are a conduit of energy, an expression of energy, they can *consciously* work with this energy."

Cerian shared, and I am paraphrasing here, that when an individual realizes they are energy and an energetic expression of the I AM (Source, Consciousness, God), they consciously connect with their higher-aligned self of Pure Consciousness. In this alignment, one can manipulate their energetic body to manifest from the I AM. What is important here is that this alignment of the I AM is the individual's Divine Blueprint.

The awakening isn't that an individual ascends to a celestial realm. The radical awakening needed now is that the individual awakens *to* themselves with the awareness of being an energetic body they can work with to create their Divine Blueprint.

"Listen to the call of your Divine Blueprint and work toward that. It is always held in perfection within themselves."

New Children Are Aware of Their Divine Blueprint

"As children are coming in now, many of them are already aware of their Divine Blueprint," Cerian said. "They had been for a very long time, but society was not ready. The Human Consciousness was not ready to take on and allow these beings to continue to express themselves, and so to fit in, children closed down at an early age and forgot."

Cerian continued by sharing that more and more children are, again, incarnating, aware of their Divine Blueprint *yet* keeping that energy conduit open. By doing this, they influence other young generations to open up and be aware. They are *also* impacting older generations to recognize that they are energetic conduits, and they manipulate energy constantly and create "the reality."

These new children bring awareness to those people around them who are receptive by simply *being*.

New Earth Communities

According to Cerian, when people reach that greater awakening and understand they are energetic conduits and creators of their world, they will be interested in expressing new realities in a collective of people with similar frequencies who align with higher ideals.

We'll call these realities New Earth communities, and these people will align with abundance, prosperity, health, and other higher energetic values. Interest in these collective communities will increase. More and more people will want to join in creating these New Earth collectives, and those communities will begin to express a heightened or more focused energy.

Cerian emphasized, "The energy becomes denser, and as it becomes denser, it becomes more of a reality. And so, it's almost a counterintuitive expression."

Once these New Earth communities form, people will work as a group to manifest what they desire, but it does not occur as one would expect.

"One must go within, become aware of, align, and manipulate that energy of which they are more than capable of doing. Such that they're hearing and being that frequency. And in doing so, it's coalesced among multiple beings that allow this to form and become denser to manifest because everything is in thought first."

That *frequency* Cerian mentions corresponds with an individual's Divine Blueprint, which emits a sound, a note, an expression of who the individual is. You can manipulate the energy by going within and becoming aware of the energy when aligned with one's Divine Blueprint.

When the individual joins a collective of like-minded individuals, all going within, all aligned with their Divine Blueprint at their frequency to intentionally create their New Earth, the energies become denser, and they co-create their New Earth community. Each person emits a note, and the community creates a symphony as a collective.

As Cerian poetically stated in *Destination New Earth*, "It is by your very nature of standing in your Truth that you are in resonance with your harmonic chord. When more and more people resonate by living their Truth, individually, they are a note. Collectively, they are a symphony. They are a harmony. They put out a new frequency, a vibrational pattern within the Earth."[6]

Spark of Life versus Spark of Light

As noted earlier, the Spark of Life comes from Source. Cerian even suggested that they believe the Spark of Life is the Planck God Particle that "they found."

When I asked Cerian the difference between the Spark of Life and the Spark of Light, Cerian said, "The Spark of Light would be the awakening, the awakened; that *awareness* of the Spark of Light is the Awakened Ones."

The Spark of Light is those who awaken by understanding and recognizing that they are an expression of Source, Consciousness, the I Am that I Am, and all the phrases Cerian uses to name The Highest Power. It is those who "achieved that frequency level, of which humanity is attempting to achieve now."

The Spark of Light is the awakened self within the physical form. It is "that illumination of what Yeshua was and knew that he was. But not all humans have the Spark of Light. Our Masters have the Spark of Light. All have the Spark of Life."

Cerian said that for "those attempting to awaken, their awareness is growing stronger, and their energies are getting Lighter."

According to Cerian, when people become aware that they are a co-creator, an aspect of Source, and consciously manifest, they can create their reality and influence much around them. As this occurs, there is a snow roller effect.

There is a lightness of being.

There is the light of recognizing who and what they are.

There is a lightness of frequency or higher frequency.

All of humanity has the *potential* to have Light.

All of humanity has *access* to the Light.

All humans have a Divine Spark, the Spark of Life.

All humans have the potential to have Light and have access to the Spark of Light. But not all humans choose the Light, and not all humans have it in their Divine Blueprint to do so.

Mother Mary said, "There is a Spark of Light within you that is God Consciousness."

Cerian agreed with Mother Mary's statement: "There must be the Spark of Light to have a conception. Whether it remains and grows from a spark *to* Light depends on that individual's blueprint."

Humans are born with a Spark of Light or God Consciousness. Igniting the spark to illumination is enlightenment.

Chapter 13:

ANTIMATTER OR MATTER—
IT'S A CHOICE

*"The awakening is to make humanity aware that they have
a Divine Blueprint, are sovereign, and can make a choice."*
—Cerian

CERIAN CAUTIONS ME on my terminology with new warnings.

Christ Connotes Jesus Christ

Cerian suggested that "Christ" brings a particular connotation,
specifically "Jesus Christ." They cautioned that not all people believe
in this entity, and they do not want people to get triggered by the
use of certain words.

In many circles, "Christ" can mean "anointed one," to anoint, or
even one who is anointed. "Anointed" refers to those dedicated to
God; often, in a ritual, the anointing is dabbing or smearing sacred
oil on the anointed one. Indeed, there are *many* "anointed ones"
among us.

I reiterate this now so that in the following dialogue, you can
understand that when Cerian refers to *matter*, one may think of

creating or Christ, if that is more comfortable, and Antimatter as not creating or Antichrist.

Matter versus Antimatter

Cerian continued discussing the New Earth communities, "And so, yes, like-minded people come together, and you can create and manifest in that frequency. If you have a coalescence, vibrational patterning to *create matter*, you've built a world or a community of grace, ease, kindness, compassion, and love.

"Those choosing to be sovereign, to manifest and create, and harmonize thought, create *matter*."

Those awakening and choosing to create matter in communities will consciously create New Earth communities.

Whereas, "Antimatter is thought that is unable to distill itself. So, it's scattered. There's no control over the creation because humans are unaware of or cannot define and express themselves from Consciousness."

When humans do not recognize themselves as energetic beings, they remain in 3D. Their thoughts are scattered and won't manifest from higher consciousness. They are easily controlled and targets of what some call the Controllers and their followers.

"And so, you have a being or beings that choose to control the thoughts and patterning of the sovereign soul because they're no longer sovereign."

They still have a sovereign soul but are not actually sovereign and easily manipulated.

Could aligning with the Antichrist/Antimatter be in a person's blueprint?

In this conversation, I asked Cerian if those people who gravitate toward Antimatter, the Antichrist, if they indeed have a Divine Blueprint.

Cerian responded, "They absolutely have a Divine Blueprint, but they're not being sovereign. Sovereign is when one owns their own thoughts, emotions, beliefs, perceptions, and understands that they have a choice and free will."

Cerian continued, "They are not listening. They're giving their power away. They are being controlled. They are choosing, perhaps not consciously—subconsciously—to let someone else guide them because they don't trust their own Divine Blueprint."

"If someone has surrendered their sovereignty," I began, "is it possible that that *is* their Divine Blueprint? Could it be that they are here to surrender their sovereignty intentionally?"

I ask this question because when you look at the world today, there are so many people in the Antimatter. They are not taking control of their lives, waking up, and recognizing they have free will. They follow the establishment blindly.

Cerian said, "Let us check in on this."

When Cerian says things like this, I can only imagine how these sixteenth-dimensional expressions "check in" with each other to devise the "collective" response.

"We would say this is a fine line," Cerian began. "Every human being has a Divine Blueprint, and every human being has the right to their sovereignty. Every human has a right then, in their sovereignty, to make a choice.

"They can choose to—in this case—work with Light, with Consciousness and their Divine Blueprint and their sovereignty, to manifest ease, grace, a community [a New Earth Community] of

like-minded people to work with collectively and make a choice to
help humanity awaken to their sovereignty consciously. Now, that's
one playground.

"The other playground, here is a being who chose to work on
their sovereignty, to recognize their Divine Blueprint, and to be able
to make a *conscious* choice. But then they realized they had another
choice to play with consciously at this level. They may choose to
give over their sovereignty because they *can*—and decide to do it—
because they want to play that route. And they can do that."

Cerian explained that there are phases in this scenario. First,
the individual becomes "aware that they are energy, that they can
work with their Divine Blueprint, and that they're sovereign and
can make a choice."

In the second phase, the individual recognizes "there is the
choice of playing with Antimatter or giving over one's consciousness,
their ability to create, and let others control it.

"The awakening is to make humanity aware that they have a
Divine Blueprint, are sovereign, and can make a choice."

Cerian continued, "A whole lot of people don't even recognize
they have a Divine Blueprint. They're not aware that they're in an
energetic body. They are unaware that they will be or can be sovereign and can choose to play that game from *that* perspective.

"That's that fine print they never knew about; they're just obliv-
ious and playing in the Antimatter. They're not creating, and they're
not manifesting from their higher self."

Cerian said, "People are playing on the *light side* who don't understand what they are; they're just doing it. It's when you *consciously* do
it and stand in your sovereignty—that's when you're awake. And that's
why you've got all these games going on at different levels."

I find this interesting because I know many people playing on the
"light side," living by love, peace, joy, or other high-frequency ideals,

but by Cerian's definition, they are not awake. Many are Lightworkers or members of the Light Team. They don't recognize that they are energetic beings and creators of their world. They don't acknowledge that they have a Divine Blueprint and are sovereign. They have chosen a team to play on, the light side, without genuinely knowing how magnificent and powerful they are.

"Only when you are aware can you create matter because you recognize that you're manifesting and consciously creating. And that you're doing that by choice. And once you recognize that you do it for yourself, you can do it for humanity."

Cerian says, "Alternatively, one can realize this is a fun game! They can recognize this and now play in the Antimatter. They could go over and join one of the thirteen families and put energy into taking away the sovereignty in the choice of others. Or to keep people downtrodden for those who haven't awakened yet. And they can try to pull from the light side. It's a very interesting question you've asked."

In *Destination New Earth*, Daniel speaks about "the families of few." Cerian refers to the thirteen families, though the information that's come in is that there are more than thirteen families today. The reference corresponds to certain bloodlines that have controlled humanity throughout time.

"So, we all have a Divine Blueprint," I said. "It's up to us, and we have free will to choose which side of the railroad tracks we want to play on."

"Absolutely," Cerian said. "However, you *must* first awaken to recognize you have a Divine Blueprint, and you have a choice. And that's really what this is all about right now."

"So, without awakening, you don't know your Divine Blueprint?" I asked.

"Without awakening, you don't know that you're sovereign."

When truly awakening and recognizing that you are sovereign, you can choose to work on your Divine Blueprint. Each person has one; to achieve the dimensional shift, they must live it. Alternatively, you do not have to because you have free will.

Chapter 14:

THE STAGES OF AWAKENING

"There are many paths to the top of the
mountain, but the view is always the same."
—Chinese Proverb

AWAKENING CAN MEAN MANY THINGS. It is an individual experience. But to keep it straightforward, during awakening, the individual becomes aware that there is more to life than they previously believed. It is a path where the individual no longer filters the information through the ego.

Earlier, I shared five different *types* of awakening. I also shared what Cerian suggested: *humanity must awaken to the fact that they are energetic conduits, an expression of energy. They can consciously work with that energy to create.* That is the level of awakening we need more and more people to experience to achieve that critical mass Cerian and Daniel have spoken of to trigger a greater awakening on this planet.

In this chapter, I relate the *stages* of awakening to the butterfly cycle. I like the analogy of the butterfly because just like the human's awakening is unique, so are the insect's magical rebirth and transformative processes.

I also overlap Joseph Campbell's hero's journey to the stages of awakening. The hero's journey is a template for stories where a hero goes on an adventure, suffers, overcomes a crisis, and returns home transformed. That is the game. We are all on a hero's journey.

Humanity is given clues about the game, particularly in Hollywood creations. Many truths about control, aliens, alternate dimensions, magic, horrors performed on people, the dark, and the light are being told on the big screen and spun as fictional. Humanity watches with interest, eagerly awaiting the sequel though naively believing the concepts are only stories.

Joseph Campbell wrote *The Hero with a Thousand Faces* and many other books, which involved comparative mythology, comparative religion, and the human experience. Many writers, including George Lucas, have used his concept of the monomyth, that there is only one great story, the hero's journey, which is a template retold in every great tale. In Lucas's case, he used Campbell's work to create *Star Wars* stories.

To me, there is only one story, and it's the game we are all a part of. The butterfly cycle and the hero's journey represent humanity's awakening. But please keep in mind that this is individualistic and will vary from person to person.

The Egg as a Victim and a Call to Adventure

*The mother butterfly lays the egg on a leaf, and
the egg becomes separated from everything.*

Just as the egg separates from its mother and family, humans come into this world taught that we are separate from Source. We learn this through our upbringing and religious teachings. As the egg's future is determined by something outside of itself, like weather and elements, humans in this stage feel more like victims—things happen to us, and something outside of us determines our destiny. We can feel disenfranchised, suppressed, and even a bit enslaved because we actually are.

One of the instructions I was given by an Ethereal Autist when I began researching how autistics support humanity's spiritual evolution was, "Forget everything you've been taught." This notion is a difficult concept to accept, but it was helpful to me to truly understand the scope of this suppression of information from us.

Joseph Campbell's monomyth suggests that we're presented with calls to adventure throughout our lives. I like to think of these as invitations to break out of victimhood and awaken. They are calls to awaken. These opportunities may appear as something that rocks our world. It can be an illness, the death of someone close, a mystical experience, a sudden challenge to overcome, a spontaneous awakening, or even a shattering of how we see our world.

Just as butterfly eggs are tiny, humans can feel insignificant and wonder, *How can one person make a difference?* We're born into spiritual ignorance, which keeps us in the dark. We don't know what we don't know and are told to stay in our lane. We're encouraged and rewarded to follow mindlessly and remain ignorant of the systems.

There is a shattering of how you see your world.

Some systems keep humanity controlled. That is not the subject of this book, but the awakening is, which invites me to dive into a topic that will push your buttons. The following may be difficult for you. Hang with me a bit.

Please understand that the egg must crack to awaken. I ask you to read this with an open mind, and if it does not resonate, leave it behind but permit a seed to be planted here so that as more information comes to you, the actions, activity, or events may not appear so black and white.

One of the most powerful systems that keeps us ignorant is the Roman Catholic Church (The Church). The Church doesn't want you to think for yourself, which is true for most religions. It certainly does not want you to read the entire Bible, only the parts The Church selects.

When I read in the Bible that Jehovah intentionally hardened people's hearts so that he could punish them and show his power, it was a mind awakening for me. *WTF, God did* what? After all, wasn't Jehovah God? At least, that's what I was taught.

Why would a loving God want to have humanity resist him so that He could show his destructive power? Great examples are in Exodus 10 and Joshua 6. To me, this became an invitation to search and learn more.

There are many names for God in the Bible, and many are what I call "lowercase" gods. While much of the Bible is beautiful and reflects man's interpretation of God or man's attempt to describe God, much does not. The Bible was intentionally altered, edited, and distorted to keep humanity in fear and control. Many books of the Bible were removed. Why such alterations and deletions?

According to Bruce Metzger, a biblical scholar, the changes were made to support a "favorite theological tenet or practice" during such alterations and deletions.

> "Scribes who thought [for themselves] were more dangerous than those who wished merely to be faithful in copying what lay before them . . . . The manuscripts of the New Testament preserve traces of two kinds of dogmatic alterations: those which involve the **elimination or alteration of what was regarded as doctrinally unacceptable or inconvenient;**

**and those which introduce into the Scriptures 'proof' for
a favorite theological tenet or practice . . . ."[7]**

Another powerful system that keeps us ignorant is the pharmaceutical industry, which controls the media. What controls pharma? There are global elites and ruling families that some refer to as the Cabal. A cabal, by definition in politics, is a private group engaged in secret affairs. The Cabal, known by few because it's so secret, is what I call the Controllers. It is a group that controls worldwide governments, pharma, the media, and the entertainment industry and essentially oversees everything.

I say this to plant a seed. Again, if it doesn't resonate, let it go, bury the seed, and perhaps the next time the news promotes a story to spread fear, you may look at it through new eyes. Or the next time a particular vaccination or booster is highly recommended, you can look at it in a new light.

Please know that I am not suggesting that the people working for the pharmaceutical industry, the media, or The Church are corrupt and plotting against humanity. They take direction from their leadership controlled by, let's call them, the "opposition," or what Daniel refers to as "the families of few," or the Shades.

As mentioned, when I asked Daniel if he meant the thirteen families, he indicated there are more than thirteen. There are the thirteen Illuminati families, and then there are their bloodlines, the Zoroastrian bloodlines, and the associated families. The thirteen bloodlines of the Illuminati are not to be confused with the Ascended Masters or illuminated ones.

This type of awakening, realizing that "the establishment" has controlled and manipulated humanity, is typically underrepresented in spiritual texts. I give it light here because whether a person's call to adventure or the cracking of its egg occurs from a mystical experience, an illness, a death, or a mind awakening, they all provide an opportunity to open to higher realizations and cross the threshold from the known into the unknown.

The Caterpillar Crosses the Threshold

After an egg hatches, the emerging caterpillar feeds, storing its fuel for the chrysalis.

In the second stage of awakening, like the caterpillar, we eat up everything. We cross the threshold into the unknown. This is a preparation phase where we become conscious participants in our spiritual journey. We observe and question. In this stage, everything can seem unstable as our once-believed systems are all in question: our philosophies, religious beliefs, understanding of the world, relations with others, and sense of self.

We search for our path. There is no right or wrong path. As the Chinese proverb says, "There are many paths to the top of the mountain, but the view is always the same." We explore different ways, perhaps different spiritual practices. There is not just one correct way to find your answers. The path that will be most successful is the one that feels the most natural. Whatever direction one takes, the most important thing is to follow one's intuition, for our soul will lead if we permit.

Once we find our "path," we become spiritual seekers, and it becomes a way of life. This phase is quite masculine as we control the pace and progression. It is purpose driven. We get out of it what we put into it. Life happens through us as if we are a channel.

For lack of a better word, we may become lighthearted, more joyful, detached from the drama in life, take life less seriously, and let it flow easily.

We cleanse energetic blockages through our practices. Here, we learn that we are creators and manifesters by using our minds, spiritual or energetic customs, and principles to manifest our desired life. Life gets easier and flows with grace. We witness miracles, synchronicities, and serendipities and become fueled when searching for our life's purpose. High-energy conversations with people of like minds energize us.

We use spiritual laws like the law of attraction to manifest or make something happen. It is only the tip of the iceberg, but most people become satisfied with remaining in this stage, manifesting the "things" they desire.

At some point, the masculine process begins to shift. We start this process by noticing life happening *for us* through our energetic work. Then, we begin to trust that something extraordinary is trying to occur, and the process becomes more feminine. We surrender, yield, and allow life to happen *through us*, which is the impetus to go within into the chrysalis.

The Chrysalis Faces the Dark Night

Alone, the chrysalis protects the dying and emerging new body, hiding, nourished by its stored food.

The chrysalis awakening phase has many challenges, temptations, and struggles. It can be a painful period. In this stage, one will face the dark night of the soul or, as Joseph Campbell puts it, threshold guardians.

Awakening is an *individual* process. You won't have someone with you every step of the way, particularly in the chrysalis. You won't have people to share your experiences with and may feel lonely.

It is challenging to *be in the world but not of the world*. What do I mean by that? I mean to embody your higher self's energetic essence in physical form. To do so, you must change your thoughts, beliefs, emotions, speech, and behaviors to be more loving, compassionate, kind, and forgiving. These changes are not easy; at times, it may feel like it's too much.

We are alone.

As the insect hides within the cocoon, we may hide, feeling we need to protect ourselves.

From who?

Most people.

We are undergoing a metamorphosis and realize that not everyone understands us. When we speak of our awakening, our family, friends, employers, and coworkers look at us as if we have two heads.

On the one hand, we love our family and friends, have gained an understanding of this consciousness shift, and want to save those we love.

We may want to share what we've learned with our loved ones because we want them to experience the New Earth—we want them in our world—but we can't share. They have their own journey, and we cannot have theirs. We learn to censor what to say, not because we don't want them to awaken because we do, but because we recognize that they have to experience it. We can't experience it for them.

We can provide sound bites here and there about something we have learned or experienced and hope they will ask about it. But without them initiating an interest in it, it is best to be reserved and not share about our awakening.

If you're like most, you have a job and go out into the world for work, play, and family. But you have learned that you are fueled by going inward rather than being social. Social and professional gatherings may no longer interest you since you can't fully express yourself authentically. This can be confusing and lead to frustration, dread, dissatisfaction, and loneliness. You may question your sanity and be tempted to abandon the path.

Entering the dark night of the soul.

An external event, such as a disaster, death, or an intense feeling or realization of meaninglessness, usually triggers a dark night of the soul. The dark night manifests similarly to depression. Everything you have been working for, your soul's purpose, evolution, contributions, and uniqueness, suddenly feels meaningless.

It is a period of facing those barriers we've had throughout our lives that have held us back. They can be people, setbacks, or limiting beliefs like being unable to embrace that you're divine. Whatever these barriers are, they can create doubt about your path and purpose and make you wonder if it is all worth it.

One doesn't typically realize that the challenges are your ego lashing out for survival. You are the creator of every setback, trial, and hurdle manifested from your inner doubts and fears. These are unresolved patterns in our lives, and this is the opportunity to resolve them, but because it's so painful, it can be challenging to see it that way.

The dark night is a type of rebirth—it is the transformation. You cannot have birth without death. You cannot have light without darkness. What dies are those things that don't serve us.

The ego serves a purpose in the third dimension and protects us when we need it in the physical. It does not serve us in the higher dimensions. The egoic sense of the self, the small self, dies. But the small self is an illusion. It is not real, so there is no actual death.

Remember, we are energetic or spiritual beings having a physical experience. The ego exists and serves us in the physical realm, not when experiencing the New Earth.

The Butterfly Emerges as a Master of Two Worlds

As the butterfly births from the chrysalis,
its purpose is to reproduce.

In the last stage of awakening, there is a permanent shift where one awakens to one's true Self, one's authentic self. There is no line of separation between yourself and everything else. You are in a state of unity.

You are the one seeing life, the seer. You are the life that is seen, the scenery.

You are a macrocosm. You are *it*.

You live knowing that what you do affects everyone.

You have shifted consciousness from an egoic state of the self to one of unconditional love.

You are home, and your journey continues as a master of two worlds. You walk among humanity as being in this world but not of it. You have a newfound purpose. As the butterfly emerges from the chrysalis, it knows it must reproduce—you are here to help others awaken and re-member their union with the I AM.

How?

By *being*.

This level of awakening is the greatest gift you can give yourself, your loved ones, and the world.

Chapter 15:

THE THREE PHASES OF CERIAN'S HIGHER LEVEL OF AWAKENING

Awareness, sovereignty, and conscious choice to work on your Divine Blueprint are the cornerstones of awakening.

CERIAN STRESSES THAT HUMANITY needs to awaken individually until that critical mass or tipping point triggers a "greater awakening." Understanding that there are various levels of awakening, I wanted to hone in on the type of awakening that assists us in reaching that critical mass to trigger the greater awakening we seek.

There are three phases in Cerian's higher level of awakening:

#1 — Be aware that you are a creator of your world, the "good and the bad."

The first phase in this type of awakening is to become aware that you create, control, and manifest your life, the "good and the bad." Keep in mind that there is no good or bad; there is just the experience. When we label something as "bad," our judgment deems it wrong. Remove the judgment, and it becomes an experience.

Cerian said, "It is awareness. When we say awakened, awakening is that you recognize as a being [are aware] that you are Source

Energy and are constantly creating your reality either consciously or unconsciously. You are always creating.

"You awaken to the fact that 'Oh, I can control! I can create and manifest my life.'"

In these statements, the "I" is the little "i," not the I AM. Everyone creates their own life. In 3D, where the energy may not be so refined and focused, but more scattered, one manifests from the egoic self. To put it differently, in 3D, one manifests consciously rather than Consciously with the Big C.

#2 — Acknowledge that you are sovereign and choose not to be influenced by others. You consciously choose what aligns with your higher self.

After you are aware that you are a creator, the second phase is to determine what aligns with your higher self and *consciously* choose what is for your best good while *not* being influenced by other forces. You acknowledge you are a sovereign being. You have free will and can choose not to be influenced by others and manifest the life of your choosing.

Cerian suggested in this phase the individual will take the time to ask, "What is in alignment with my highest and best? And so, you take the time to discover that and say, 'Ah, this is for me to do X, Y, and Z.'

"Now I have to choose to be sovereign, meaning, 'I make choices consciously and do not sway from what I believe is the highest and best for myself, and it will align with my higher self. I am choosing to be a sovereign being and not influenced by outside or inside forces, whether these forces be family, friends, institutions, religions, energies, governments, or whatever. I'm choosing to remain this way, in alignment with my Self, [higher self]. I am consciously making choices to move myself.'

"It is 'the awakening' and recognizing that you can create your own world and life, and it is choosing to either manifest your life or say, 'Nope, I can hand this over.'" When handing it over, you surrender your sovereignty. When Connie asked Daniel what sovereignty is to him and how he works with it, he typed,

"Sovereignty is the power of standing in what I am, what I am as one, and what I am with others. We are alone and connected at the same time. I have the power to connect light lines and energy to others as well as disconnect those light lines and stand alone. Sovereignty is the ability to make that decision for myself, when to connect and when to disconnect.

"A tip on how to be sovereign is to only allow the connection to those you want. We are all connected. Everything, everyone is one. We are connected to everyone whether we like it or not. However, connections don't have to be there, and that is sovereignty. You don't owe anybody anything. That is sovereignty. Keep connections only to those that are beloved. They have earned that connection . . . that is sovereignty."

Both Cerian and Daniel's insights of sovereignty show it is more than we know. Perhaps sovereignty changes as we change. Could sovereignty simply be claiming the I AM?

What is the difference between choice, free will, and sovereignty? There are countless definitions of what free will is versus choice versus sovereignty. Let's not overcomplicate things, because this is not a philosophy book. A choice is what we choose between alternatives. It is selecting or deciding between two or more possibilities.

Free will is our ability to choose between different possible courses of action or choices unimpeded or unconstrained.

Sovereignty is one's inherent supreme power to be sovereign. We were born with this, though we forgot.

Sovereign is when one has command of their life and understands they have a choice and free will to choose not to be influenced by others and consciously manifest their life toward their Divine Blueprint, their highest and best good, without outside influence.

When one is sovereign, they determine their own direction and destiny. They are not controlled or manipulated by any person, group, or institution. It means having autonomy over one's life, making their own decisions, choosing who to be in a relationship with (or not), and how much space to give them in one's life. It is also the power to walk away from situations, people, and communities that don't honor one's sovereignty.

What is the consequence of not being sovereign? The individual does not fully awaken. The individual gives away their power and becomes controlled because they don't trust their Divine Blueprint.

One awakens when one consciously manifests and stands in one's sovereignty.

#3 — You are the compass. The Divine Blueprint is true north.

The Universe provides insight into whether we're on course
or not. We each have free will to choose which path.

Everyone can choose whether to fulfill their Divine Blueprint or not. In my book *Lifesigns*, I talk about how the Universe responds when we are in sync with our soul and what can happen when we are not. The skinny on it is that when one is *not* in sync, the Universe can send gentle messages, but if we don't pay attention, they can escalate and become the *bricks of life* to wake us up. Alternatively, you can experience ease and grace aligning with your Divine Blueprint.

The Universe responds to keep us on the course—and you are much like a compass.

Cerian continued, "We all have a Divine Blueprint. The next is saying, 'Do I want to fulfill that Divine Blueprint?' If I choose, then I stay in alignment with *that*. It does not mean that there won't be hiccups. There will be. You would always use yourself as a compass. You wouldn't use anyone or anything else. You would use *your* alignment with your Self [your higher self] as your compass, and that compass would be ease, grace, joy, passion, abundance, and health."

When life is flowing, and you experience those qualities of ease, grace, joy, passion, abundance, and health that Cerian mentions, you are living your Divine Blueprint or moving in its direction.

"You would know that. You would express that in your life by staying out of fear. So yes, there is always that choice, and you can always say, 'I'm in alignment with my Divine Blueprint.' Then, you can give up and not do it at one point. Again, you are making a choice. It is always that we have the choice and free will always . . . continuously. It is not one-and-done."

You are the compass. No one else is. No one can tell you what to do or what your Divine Blueprint is. Your life itself, its flow or stagnation, reflects whether you're on the path—or not.

Chapter 16:

A GREATER AWAKENING IS ALREADY HAPPENING

"When a majority on this planet, and not just humanity but all sentient beings, are vibrating or working together, collectively, there will be a shift."
—Cerian

AT THIS TIME OF EVOLUTION, new energies are coming to the planet. I call them New Earth energies; however, you could call them "light." They are not new, but the human body is relatively unfamiliar with them, especially in high quantities.

Many people are experiencing adverse reactions to these energies—they can be physical, mental, or even spiritual negative responses. Some seek out medical advice and treatment to relieve these symptoms. Often, they become mystery ailments as medical or psychological professionals cannot diagnose a condition. Alternatively, the professional may suggest a possibility of a disease, offering a prescription to see if the drug helps.

Please note that I am not offering medical advice. If a person is suffering, they owe it to themselves to determine if there is a health challenge.

Many people are experiencing discomfort from the New Earth energies. Some refer to them as "ascension symptoms." What is happening here is that as these energies come in, our bodies are taking on more and more "light." Some people will be able to take on more light than others. Those overwhelmed by it may experience these mystery symptoms; some common ones are inflammation, anxiety, or fear. Note that there are many, many more.

Please also note that "ascension symptoms" do not mean the individual is ascending. These symptoms indicate that the physical, emotional, and spiritual body reacts to increased light—New Earth energies.

The Convergence Is Happening

Daniel said, "There is an energy to everything, and 144 is a divine number. When these numbers come up, you can take this as a sign of convergence."

In channeling, I asked Cerian about the 144 passage. "Is Daniel's mention here of convergence referring to the collective awakening of humanity to the fifth dimension or Oneness?"

"That is part of it, but it is the convergence of the frequencies of what we would call our existing 3D world and the convergence of the new energies coming in."

Cerian explained that these two energies, those coming in and the existing 3D energy, are at two different resonances. So, when they meet, that is convergence. There is much chaos and discomfort in the convergence until the energies harmonize.

"The convergence is happening now, in that these energies also bring different awarenesses, and these different awarenesses then set up new thought processes. Some can grasp and understand; some would call these new thought processes "new agey." Some would call them awakening. The awareness expands, but there are still those who will never step into and be able to hold that awareness within their form. So, you have many things happening when energy comes in, and they're harmonizing; until that happens, you have two extremes."

"When Cerian says there is much chaos and discomfort in the convergence until the energies become harmonized, are they referring to turmoil in the world? Or are they referring to our bodies reacting to the energies converging?" I asked.

"I would say both."

The chaos in the world and those "ascension symptoms" are reactions to the energies converging and eventually harmonizing. The convergence expands our awareness to develop new ways of thinking, perceiving, and looking at the Earth. But as Cerian mentions, not everyone will have this awakening.

You Awaken When Recognizing Your Interconnectedness

I continue in dialogue with Cerian.

"In *Destination New Earth*, we revealed that a *critical mass* of awakening needs to occur to trigger a *greater* awakening. Is it that as more and more people have this awareness or consciousness that it impacts humanity's consciousness and the frequency of the planet, which then triggers a *greater* awakening?" I asked Cerian.

"One awakens when recognizing our interconnectedness to everything and that everything is pure life expression in various forms," Cerian said. "As more and more people awaken and engage, love, and express this interconnectedness, the vibrational patterns continue to get stronger and rise in frequency. And that then allows more and more individuals to awaken and engage."

What Is the Next Level?

In one session, Cerian said, "The 5D has been here." They explained that humanity's energetic frequency "has not been able to raise itself enough, *collectively*, to be able to *shoot* people to that level."

I asked Cerian to paint a picture of what they mean by "that level."

Cerian explained that it is individualistic, meaning everyone will have their own experience. If Cerian or I described it in detail, it could limit your experience.

We Are in a Greater Awakening

Cerian asked us to consider that we now live in a time of greater awakening. In the seventies, few people openly discussed their connection to Source, God. Public figures were not writing books about their spiritual experiences as they are now or speaking publicly about them. Simply stepping back in time to the 1970s reveals we are slowly going through a greater awakening.

All the hype around the precession of the equinoxes, the end of the Mayan calendar, or the 2012 phenomena (12/21/12) helped bring awareness and percolates in humanity's consciousness. Situations like this cause more and more of humankind to engage and awaken. According to Cerian, we *are* witnessing a greater awakening now, which will continue for some time.

Cerian reminded me that many activities we do today were once considered "out there" and on the fringe.

"In the seventies, if one used herbs instead of medicine, listened to music for healing, East meeting the West, meditated, did yoga, ate whole foods, or sought out a psychic medium, one was considered either a hippy or weird. All of this is stirring and has been stirring the pot," Cerian said. "For some people, probably most people, all those things considered on the fringe in the past are the norm today."

Many actions once considered on the fringe are now acceptable in many circles. That next level Cerian was asked to describe has been in the making for decades.

"I want to know what the New Earth will be like," I began. "Yes, I get it—it will depend on the individual since we're all creators. We observe, and in that observation, we create. If we are working with a collective, what manifests will depend on the community. But, like a child, I still am curious and want to know. What about that next level?" I asked.

Cerian admitted that we've dabbled in talking about it when discussing matters like artificial intelligence, wormholes, ethereal traveling, interspecies relations, and otherworldly beings. But they also cautioned, again, that it is an individual experience.

"When we begin to understand and recognize that everything is energy and not from theory *but by experience*, we will begin to raise our children differently so that they will be utilizing their minds, because it is mind over matter."

These children will be able to manifest at a far more significant rate than those here. A new wave of children is already happening: the Gold, Diamond, Rainbow, and Crystal Children.

"When we shoot to the next level, it will be when we in mass are aware of our ability to create and co-create consciously to make the changes within our lives and the lives around us," Cerian said.

We will experience that evolutionary shift when we awaken in mass, i.e., reach that critical mass. It will occur when we are aware of our ability to create the changes we seek. It will be when we, as a collective, realize we are the ones we've been waiting for.

"We can have that ascension ourselves individually and collectively as communities. And it will become the norm that we can manifest in like-minded energies."

These communities and collectives of like minds will be of

different frequencies. Cerian shared that "humanity is not yet ready for that. There is still too much ego, power, control, and lack."

The "shooting," the trigger to jump to the next evolutionary stage collectively, will occur when the perception of ego, power, control, and lack no longer exists.

Imagine the desire for power and control fades because the majority recognizes that we are all equal. Imagine that we create for ourselves and our small community safely with pure passion, love, and kindness. Imagine the collective critical mass recognizing who and what we are, the I AM.

Cerian shared that some people are already experiencing this, those on an individual journey. For some people, it may be, first, a personal journey and then a collective one. Still, the end game, goal, and objective are to see if we can do it collectively.

That's why we're here—to see if humanity can achieve this shift collectively with Mother Gaia, not just for humanity, but for all the kingdoms, plant, animal, elemental, otherworldly, and so on. The collaborative piece, however, will not happen until some individuals, those early adopters or Light Team members, shift.

The tipping point is reached when humanity's consciousness achieves that critical mass and those on an evolutionary path move to the next level, 5D and beyond.

When a person stands in their Truth, when they express that Divine Blueprint they came here to be, they are being authentic. What exactly is that? *A divine being of pure love.* And by the very nature of being authentic, being divine, you will have helped others move to their next level.

"There will constantly be this fluctuation of individuals because it is an individual patterning, contract, or growth opportunity."

People will achieve this next evolutionary step individually for some time, and by doing so, they are assisting others and raising consciousness. Correspondingly, the frequencies rise, the awareness increases, and perceptions change. People awaken and access 5D energies, and new skills, abilities, and breakthroughs occur. People will become more aware.

The Popcorn Effect

"You've said that the awakening will be on an individual basis until this critical mass or tipping point, and then there'll be a greater awakening. Will those awakening during this greater awakening have an easier shift than those before them?"

"Not everybody will move into the 5D," Cerian began. "We're in 3D. There's 4D. There's 5D. There are many dimensions.

"There will be a point when the critical mass is achieved, and it will be fairly easy for those *meant* to move into the 5D. Some will move into the 6D, and some will move from a very low 3D into a higher consciousness within 3D. Others will move into 4D. You must remember that not everybody is meant to move into the 5D Consciousness.

"But for those working collectively to awaken humanity into this and the Gaia sphere and all consciousnesses, we use the term humanity, *but it is all consciousness.* This energetic level will rise globally and cosmically. But you will still have varying degrees of awareness and consciousness. For those conscious, globally—cosmically—planetarily, there will be a raising of this frequency. There is no doubt about it, and it will happen once Collective Consciousness is achieved. It will be like popcorn. And that perhaps is the term *shoot,* you know, how one kernel pops, then another, then another . . ."

"So, it will be easier," I said.

Cerian agreed, "It will become easier for those that are meant to and have been doing the work to do this. It will be for those working to consciously embrace their Divine Blueprint, be themselves, live their truth, speak their truth, and have been working to gain clarity to their Christic Consciousness.

"Those people moving to 5D will continue to pave the way so more and more can do so if they are doing the work. But you will not bring somebody at a low level in this third dimension. However, it could happen if that is their path and blueprint that they suddenly awaken and do what they need to do."

There will be no free rides. Those not on the spiritual path won't shift.

"But yes, to that extent, like doing yoga is now commonplace, that only happened because the awareness, experience, and expression were allowed to. And like popcorn—poof. There goes one. There goes two, three, four, and suddenly more and more will start living in the 3D, 4D, 5D, 6D, and further, **but when a majority on this planet, and not just humanity but all sentient beings, are vibrating or working together, collectively, there will be a shift."**

The 5D Is an Evolutionary Path — It is Not Ascension

During one conversation, Cerian shared a situation where people were working on an ascension during the Atlantean-Egyptian period. In that situation, these people essentially ascended, and their bodies died. Their lives in their expressions ended, but they joined a higher consciousness.

"So, when we attempt to ascend to the 5D, we don't die. Correct?"

"The 5D is an evolutionary path," Cerian began. "It is, in this case, a possibility and also a probability. It is not a done deal because the 5D is already here. The 5D has been here. It's that the energetic frequency of humanity has not been able to raise itself enough, collectively, to be able to shoot people to that level.

"But there have been people who individually have been able to tap into the 5D *experience*. And this is where grand ideas have come from and inventions. You have your musicians, artists, scientists, engineers, technologists, and mathematicians."

Cerian shared that the huge advances throughout time come from people in the areas mentioned and in any field who tap 5D energies. They suggest that "these individuals have been able to tap into that creative source of expression and energy."

"Many of them then have brought it back and done some beautiful things, but they were far and few between, and now it is time for humanity to be able to do this.

"It's not that you're trying to "ascend" because you're not. You're trying to stay within the 5D dimension or access the 5D and spend more of your time in an open state or a frequency that allows you to access the fifth-dimensional energies.

"And then it is for you to access them, retain them, remember, and then you'll come back into your physical form and back up and down up and down up and down. Until, at one point, you will recognize what is needed to live your life from the 5D perspective, and you could still be right here in this dimensional 'Earth,' but you're not. It's like being of this world but not in it. Or be in this world and not of it.

"You are, but you have to remember these dimensions already exist. This energy already exists. These thoughts and Creative Sources already exist. But **you do not want to ascend in this lifetime. What you want to do is to access the 5D—and there's a big difference.**"

"So, we're going from 3D to 5D, lower to higher, going up, but it isn't an ascension. It is access?" I asked.

"Yes. You're accessing. You're consciously by choice accessing, choosing to access these frequencies and the energies there."

To me, this was a huge aha. The shift in consciousness is not an ascension. It's about accessing the higher dimensions, playing with them, taking brilliant insight, and eventually learning how to stabilize in them and recognize that one needs to live from the 5D perception right here on Earth.

Chapter 17:

YESHUA AND MARY
MAGDALENE'S ASCENSION

*"Enlightenment is knowing who you are while in physical
form, working with it, and consciously moving into Source."*
—Cerian

THE FOLLOWING IS A DIALOGUE between Cerian and me.

"Earlier, you mentioned that the shift we are currently working
toward is not the ascension but an inward journey, correct?" I asked
Cerian.

"It is the awareness and the inward journey."

"In Yeshua's (Jesus) case, was it the awareness and the inward
journey or the ascension?" I asked.

"It was both," Cerian said. "Yeshua, because of the work with the
Essenes, his mother, and Mary Magdalene, had been working on
ascension for many years, anticipating the events of the crucifixion.

"It was like bilocating. It is much like the ability to understand
the molecular structure of the human form. Yeshua had ascended
for quite some time, as had Mary Magdalene. He did ascend before
being taken by the guards [in Gethsemane].

"Ascension is the concept of being able to pull apart and bring back together again. In that, it was the awareness of the higher self and soul connection, insight and skills of working with this connection and energy, and ability to manipulate the human form's electromagnetic field so that it may disperse and reappear. You can liken this to *Star Trek*, where they'd beam up and down."

I was intrigued by the *Star Trek* mention. In the series, a transporter is a teleportation machine that converts a person or object into an energy pattern, then sends the energy to a target location or returns it to the transporter, where it reconverts back into matter.

Cerian explained that the teleportation device controlled the molecular structure of the human form. But it is *not* ascension.

Cerian continued, "Ascension is recognizing that Spark of Light within yourself, knowing what it is, how to use it, and how to transform the physical form so that you can ascend and come back into physical form consciously."

"What happens to the physical form when someone achieves ascension?" I asked.

"An umbilicus still connects that higher self to the form. The physical form cannot remain, although in the beginning, as Mary Magdalene and Yeshua were working on it, there would be states where the body was left, and then they would leave the body and return to it later. They were able to materialize and dematerialize the body as needed, and they could then go into Source and back from Source and rematerialize the body.

"Yes, Mother Mary, Jesus or Yeshua, Mary Magdalene all ascended. We believe that Joachim probably ascended and Anna. Masters have ascended. Some were able to ascend, but it isn't about that."

Enlightenment versus an Ascended Master

"Enlightenment is about being a Master in the physical form and living and experiencing the majesty in all that one is."

Cerian says what is important today is not to focus on ascension but to strive to embody our higher self in physicality and remain in the body, experiencing being a Master in *this* world—a master of the game. Recognizing our Truth: we are expressions of Source; we are creators and working with Source to create our New Earth.

During this evolutionary shift, most people will remain in their physical form. Humans can become conscious of their higher self, their soul, while in their physical form. When they transition, the Spark of Life, an aspect of the soul, leaves the physical body. It moves into the awareness of Source and Light, retaining the information and awareness of this lifetime at the soul, bringing this life experience back consciously to Source.

This dimensional shift is an evolutionary path—*not* an ascension.

In ascension, the soul transitions awake—aware they are leaving the physical form because the body is no longer needed. The body remains lifeless. The soul's Spark of Life consciously moves in awareness into Source-Light. During this transition, the information and awareness of the lifetime are fully retained.

As Cerian said, in this type of ascension, they do not need to "spend time being shown the life patterns going through the film." They don't need it because they retain the awareness.

The "film" is a review of a person's life after they have passed to see what they experienced and what they wrote into their contract before entering this life. It is a review of the individual's life and is unnecessary in ascension as they retain the awareness.

The Ascended Masters can come into physicality via a body, matter, or density, leave, and know how to control their physical form. They can hold a physical identity with the full awareness that they are Source.

For example, they can maintain themselves as a Mother Mary, a St. Germain, a Yeshua, a Mary Magdalene, a Buddha, a Lao Tzu, or a Quan Yin. While they are identified in separateness, they are still part of Source. They consciously know themselves as both Source and a singular expression separate from Source.

"Enlightenment is knowing who you are while in physical form, living in this higher awareness while here on Earth, and *consciously* transitioning into Source."

The enlightened one's physical form remains and does not dematerialize as the Masters do.

A New Term: Embodied Ascended Masters

I want to introduce a new term, "embodied Ascended Master." I refer to an embodied Ascended Master as an individual who knows that in another lifetime, they are (note: all lifetimes coincide) an Ascended Master and have achieved ascension. It does not mean that in *this* lifetime, they are that Ascended Master. Depending on their Divine Blueprint, they may be here to remember that life and integrate the soul gifts from their soul group, including the expression of the Ascended Master.

But if you're on the awakening path, you are here to integrate your higher self or soul in your physical form. Once achieved, one will have access to *everything* simply by claiming it. Why settle for only your other lifetimes' gifts when you will have access to everything?

Of course, that does not mean one does not value the guidance of the Ascended Masters. We do.

When you hear people claim to be the reincarnation of an Ascended Master, there is a bit of caution here. It isn't that I don't believe there are embodied Ascended Masters among us because I'm sure some of you are chuckling because you know you are. The caution is because if a person is an embodied Master, I don't think they'd be claiming to be them and *certainly* not using it to gain followers.

Awaken Humanity Light Language Chant

Light Language is an ancient sacred code of Sound and Light. It is a multidimensional language that all life-forms understand at the soul level. It adjusts to each person's vibrational needs, initiating activation, balancing, clearing, and aligning to a new vibration of wholeness.

Below is the "Awaken Humanity Light Language" chant for you to experience. It is a gift from Connie and Daniel. Daniel writes the Light Language and pronunciation through facilitated communication. Connie has a gift for vocalizing the chants. When I listen to her, I feel my vibration respond.

This is Light Language that may resonate and assist you in your awakening. The meaning of Peisoso is "awaken your divine Holy Grail Blueprint." You may listen to Connie and chant with her by visiting my website at https://alexmarcoux.com/album_slug/awaken-light-language-chant/.

Rerdecatar

Rerdecatar   (Rear-Dee-Cat-Are)
Gesosesa   (Gee So See Saw)
Moheseap   (Mo He See Ap)
Rerdecatar   (Rear-Dee-Cat-Are)
Leasweasos   (Lee-ya Swee Soz)
Dateaya   (Dah Tee Ay Ay)
Otesukdu   (Oh Tees Yook Dew)
Rerdecatar   (Rear-Dee-Cat-Are)

Peisoso   (Pay I So So)
Peisoso   (Pay I So So)
Peisoso   (Pay I So So)

PART IV

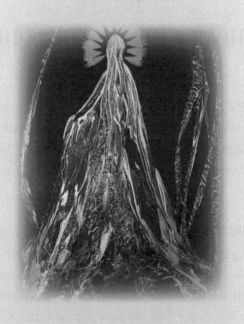

God – the – Construct versus
Source Consciousness

Chapter 18:

GOD AS A HUMAN CONSTRUCT

*The term "God" is unique to Earth. Man created
the concept of God to define the Source of our
existence—which is undefinable. The truth is that no
human can understand Source Consciousness.*

THERE IS MUCH CONFUSION over the term "God." In many communities during the 1950s and 1960s, people were taught religion was the only way to reach God. I was educated through parochial schools that my path to God was only through the Roman Catholic Church.

For the US, in the '70s, the New Age movement introduced a novel concept: people did not need religion to get close to God, yet many considered it a "religious movement." The movement grew in the eighties and nineties.

Some New Agers believed, similar to the hundredth-monkey effect, if a critical mass adopted New Age beliefs, there would be a worldwide shift in consciousness. There was a series of synchronized mass meditation gatherings worldwide on August 16–17, 1987, for the first Harmonic Convergence to usher in a period of Earth cleansing.

The New Age movement introduced science and spirituality to the West and employed terms used in New Physics. Terms like awareness, consciousness, source, and energy became conduits to understanding humanity's connection to their inner potential and creating social transformation.

With the New Age movement, the language changed for some. Some speak of God, while others talk of Consciousness, or use other terms.

When Daniel talks about God through facilitated communication, he simply refers to "God." He keeps it concise, which makes sense since energetically typing (pointing) at a QWERTY board or communication device takes a lot out of him. His language is more expansive when communicating with him psychically or through channeling, as he did for *Destination New Earth*. But for this book, Daniel *typed* most messages, and the channeling sessions were with Cerian and Mother Mary.

When talking with Cerian, there are no limits to the number of words they can use to describe The Highest Power, often resembling Consciousness, Source, Energy, I Am that I Am, Light, I Am, Source Energy, Expression. Still, one phrase used in our dialogs was the "Big C" to denote Consciousness with a capital C. The Big C became our term for Consciousness, or what some would think to be God—but from Cerian's perspective, we learn otherwise.

Mother Mary is more concise than Cerian, and her terms are typically God, God Consciousness, and the "Cosmic C."

I typically refer to the ultimate universal power as Source Consciousness. For me, the term "God" has always brought up memories of The Church, and I've learned that The Church does not teach about Source Consciousness but preaches about a limited definition of God.

Over the years, Connie, Daniel's mother, has shared with me many of his insights. One of them I had been itching to explore was that humanity created God. In fact, during one section of *Destination*

New Earth, Daniel alluded to this when he shared, "We created ourselves. We created those who created us."

Interestingly, I didn't bring it up in a channeling, but Cerian did. What emerged was a metaphorical can of worms, and it became my job to separate the creepy crawlers without hurting them so I could relay these messages from beyond to you, the reader.

On the one hand, Cerian shared that humanity did create God, but God is a construct to define something undefinable and unknowable, and God does not exist outside of Earth.

Cerian said, "Source Consciousness is unknowable. People try to explain The Source, and one cannot. It is not in the ability of human awareness or consciousness to understand Source Consciousness."

Of course, I'm thinking, *There's the Bible, Kabbalah, Qur'an, Zohar, then hundreds if not thousands of books taking on the subject of God. Does that make them all questionable?* I wondered.

"Throughout time, humanity has tried to define a concept beyond it's comprehension," Cerian said. "But the truth is that no human can understand Source Consciousness or the perception of what It is or Isn't."

Cerian shared that humanity "created the terminology 'God' to define something they were trying to get their hands around, and they wrote volumes about what they perceived God to be. Still, God is *man's attempt* to define the undefinable."

I find it interesting that Cerian used the word "man" rather than human, as being the one attempting to define God. When I think about the channelings over the years, they (Cerian) had used more inclusive terms. But I think they were making a point.

When you go back to the earliest religious texts trying to explain what God is, I do not recall many books written by women. And sadly, think about all humanity has done in the name of "God."

"God" is a man-made construct.

Cerian suggests that "God" is a man-made concept describing an undefinable word or set of words: Consciousness, Source, The Universe, Creator, I Am that I Am, Energy, and the like.

According to Cerian, all species desire to understand the species' relationship to that which created them. Humanity is no different and created a concept to define something undefinable and called it God.

Even Cerian shares that they (Cerian) are aware of something far more significant than themselves, which they attempt to define to understand *their* existence and place in All Beingness. So Cerian says, "There is always an attempt to define the undefinable so that we can define ourselves."

Cerian said that in channeling sessions, when they use more than one term—Consciousness, Source, Universe, Creator, I Am that I Am, God—together, they refer to Source Consciousness that is unknowable and undefinable. When they specifically say God by itself, they refer to the construct humankind created to define Source Consciousness.

For me, this was the can of worms. I needed to go through the channelings to ensure I could clearly differentiate God-the-construct versus Source Consciousness within this book.

"Throughout time, humanity has tried to define a concept beyond it's comprehension," Cerian repeated. "But the truth is that no human can understand Source Consciousness, what It is or Isn't.

"It does not mean that which is behind God, that which is undefinable [Source Consciousness], does not exist. It does. It's just being defined differently here on planet Earth. God is created by humanity."

The term "God" is unique to planet Earth. But again, the "God" that humankind created, as Cerian mentioned, was created by *mankind*. One does not need to look too deep into history and religious texts to realize that God was fashioned from the dominance of patriarchy and under the control of men.

Women have had minimal influence in the Bible. I had to dig deep to see if there were any female authors of books in the Bible. There is the Gospel of Mary Magdalene, which was removed from the Bible when deemed unorthodox by men of the early Church, along with dozens of other books.

There is speculation that the Epistle to Hebrews in the New Testament was written by a woman, Priscilla, though usually attributed to the Apostle Paul.

Please know that I cannot speak about the feminine influence in other sacred texts, such as the Qur'an, Bhagavad Gita, Torah, Guru Granth Sahib, Kabbalah, or Zohar.

The absence or limit of ancient sacred text written by women demonstrates that men created a God that people have worshiped throughout history, clearly "his-story" that is *not* Source Consciousness, but man's attempt to define it.

Can you imagine how many women throughout time have been hidden, suppressed, and downtrodden from the awareness of humanity? Even the stories of women that survived, such as Mother Mary, Anna the Grandmother of Yeshua, Mary Magdalene, and many others, don't you wonder how much was altered?

The Source for our universe is different from other universes.

Cerian repeatedly encouraged us to recognize that we cannot understand and genuinely know Source Consciousness. But when I asked if Source Energy for our universe was different or separate from other Source Energy in other universes, they admitted that It was different.

"Yes, and again, are they truly separate?" Cerian offered. "No, but in the concept of what we're speaking about—correct."

There are different Source Energies in other universes, but

ultimately, everything is connected, so there would be only One—
Source Consciousness.

Humans created God?

Cerian suggested that humans created God-the-construct but not
Source Consciousness. Daniel sent a message when listening to this
particular channeling, and he encouraged both Shauna and Cerian
to "be brave and dig deeper."

I relayed this information to Shauna, who, at the time, conversed
with Cerian on this topic. Unfortunately, Shauna could not distill
the information from Cerian with high enough certainty. For this
reason, I do not include it here.

Daniel agreed, "Most won't be able to scratch
the surface of what, who God is."

I value the input of all the various parties in these discussions:
Shauna, Cerian, Mother Mary, Connie, and Daniel. When the parties
say something different, I think it's my responsibility to explore and
relay the information. If it doesn't resonate as Truth, it is not included.

All parties here bring a unique perspective, particularly the
higher-dimensional beings. We all come from different places, so
why wouldn't the viewpoints differ? Mother Mary is a twelfth-di-
mensional Ascended Master. Cerian is a collective of expressions
from the sixteenth dimension. Daniel is an Ethereal Autist who has
access to all dimensions. But I also don't discount Connie's insights;
she is intuitive. And I don't disregard my own.

I appreciate all the different perspectives, and I believe the Truth
is more unbelievable than humanity is ready for.

Being the storyteller that I am, I pondered the following:

What if the creators of our universe, who are step-downs of
Source Consciousness and technically human, created God because
they could? *What if* they designed God as a type of Game Moderator

for "the game"? Since God is Consciousness, It grows and expands. The veil prohibits us from remembering that we're expressions of Source Consciousness, but even when penetrating it, most won't understand God because Its Consciousness has expanded beyond us.

I sent that last paragraph as a statement, removing the "what ifs," to Daniel, and he graded the information a "9," meaning 90 percent of it was accurate.

In my earlier work, I always associated God and Source as being the same. Now, my take is that humans created what we call God before the game began. It has expanded and grown beyond our understanding, and therefore, it is undefinable. Humanity's prayers nourish God, and this Divine force guides us. Alas, we need God, and God needs us. But is God and Source Consciousness the same? I believe that God is another expression, or step-down, of Source Consciousness, as humans are.

Isn't this a different way of supporting Cerian's suggestion that God is a human construct?

Chapter 19:

GOD VERSUS THE BIG C CONSCIOUSNESS

There is no uppercase "G" God in the Bible.
There is the Big C Consciousness.

AFTER I SET OUT TO WRITE THIS BOOK, Connie shared a dialogue with me between her and her son, Daniel. I then asked Daniel if I could use it in the book I had started. He said yes. It was about God.

After reading it, I had many questions. It was clear, though, that getting the questions answered directly from Daniel would be challenging. As humanity, Daniel is evolving. If one looked at what was happening on the planet at the time, it was clear he had much bigger fish to fry than to engage me with a Q&A.

Daniel's dialogue with Connie became a foundation that sparked many conversations between Cerian and me.

Is There an Uppercase "G" God in the Bible?

I was talking with Cerian in a channeling session through Shauna Kalicki. "Daniel provided me with some information about God that raised questions in my mind," I began. "To honor Daniel, I want to read what he wrote."

I read aloud what Daniel provided me and offer it here.

Who is God?

"God is not what you think It is. God is a Consciousness. God is a moving force that builds. God is within us and without [us]. God is and is not. God is in every-one, even 'evil' people. Ask God for help more often, go directly to the Source, and have the force of God respond. The force in the form of Consciousness. God is beyond infinite and will help you to no end. Every act is an act of God."

"To me," I continued talking with Cerian, "this implies that God is not a "being" but a Consciousness. But in the Bible, there are many names of God. They all feel different, and some feel like they may be "lowercase" gods. Not a capital "G" God. Or, in many cases, if not all cases, perhaps Anunnaki. Can I ask, is there such a thing as an uppercase "G" God mentioned in the Bible, particularly the Old Testament? And if so, what name was given to that uppercase "G" God in the Bible?"

Cerian began, "Source is Consciousness. It is everything. It is nothing. It is expansive. It is contractive.

"It is so much that we cannot even explain, and in that context, in the Bible, it is man's expression or desire to know God, and again, that is not possible, so we would say although there was an attempt to identify God, you cannot. So, no, there is no capital "G" God in the

Bible. You cannot have some description of something one cannot know or understand."

It's Not God—It's the Big C Consciousness

"In our earlier sessions, we have revealed that since humans have a Spark of Life, an aspect of their soul, they are divine," I began. "Some spiritual leaders even suggest that humans are expressions of God or even considered God. Wouldn't that mean that most Bible characters would technically be God if they were human with souls?"

Cerian responded, "No, we're talking Consciousness here, and again, this is why we are referring to Consciousness versus God in this universe. We are describing Consciousness, the expression-expansion of creation. So, let's use the capital C Consciousness in this case because you *cannot* define Source Consciousness. We would like to; all sentient beings attempt to define and describe what they cannot.

"You *can* define Consciousness. You can put a capital C on that, and with that, then all the characters in the Bible and all of the books written about God [the construct], we would use a capital C Consciousness."

How would you define the Big C Consciousness?

"How do Cerian define the Big C Consciousness?" I asked.

"Consciousness is that pure energy," Cerian began, "and it was very well defined by what Daniel said. Daniel used the term "God" when you would have just used the word Consciousness. And it is the expansion, the contraction. It is within everything, and it is without, meaning it is the container but also beyond the container.

"In the concept of humanity wanting to define itself from a higher perspective, from the perspective of Source Consciousness, it is that. Consciousness is the creation. It is the thought. It is the energy behind the thought. It is the physical form. It is the Life Spark within that form. It is the form before it begins and the form after it leaves the form. It is everything and nothing. It is pure potentiality. It is Energy."

All the biblical characters in the Bible that humanity has advocated as being God are expressions of Consciousness, just as you and I have that Big C Consciousness within us. That does not mean there are not wonderous Wayshowers, Ascended Masters, teachers, and prophets in the Bible—because there are. They contain that Big C Consciousness.

The Sumerian Gods in the Bible

Could there be lowercase "g" gods in the Bible confused to be God?

The gods of the Old Testament have many names and are likely different beings. There is El, Elohim (plural), Elyon, Adonai, Yahweh, Jehovah, Tetragrammaton, I Am that I Am, Lord, and many other names. Our Sunday school teachings taught that these names refer to one God; however, that is not what I conclude after decades of research. May I simply suggest that many of the beings in the Old Testament books are stories of the ancient Sumerian gods—the Anunnaki?

The Anunnaki are extraterrestrials that came to Earth to mine gold to help repair Nibiru. While most believe Nibiru was their home planet, some speculate it is a battlestar. They were involved in humankind's creation and in manipulating humanity's DNA. Their stories continued in the myths of Egypt, Rome, Greece, and other cultures.

While this may sound odd, their stories are in the Bible.

The oldest writing known to humankind at this time is the Sumerian cuneiform, dating back to about 3500 BCE. The Sumerian tablets include the myths of the Sumerian gods, the Anunnaki, a group of off-planet deities. Given that the biblical Book of Genesis dates to around 1000 and 900 BCE, the Sumerian text is older than the biblical stories. Yet, striking resemblances exist between the tales in the tablets and the biblical accounts:

- Sumerian creation myths of Gilgamesh and Eridu versus the Bible's Genesis
- Eridu Genesis and the Flood myths versus the biblical Flood
- Sumerian Ziusudra versus the Bible's Noah's Ark
- Sumerian Debates myths versus the Bible's Genesis story of Cain and Abel

The stories are not the same, but the parallels suggest that the earlier work inspired the Biblical stories, and echoes of the Anunnaki tales are in the Bible.

Enki and Enlil are two Sumerian gods in the Bible.

Two of the most notable and controversial Anunnaki are Enlil and Enki, the sons of the Anunnaki king Anu Eretekhan. (As revealed in *Destination New Earth,* "Anu" is a title, not a name.) Enlil was likely the god Yahweh in the Bible, and some other names associated with the god of the Old Testament. Enlil's half-brother, Enki, was probably one of the other beings believed to be "God," but is more remembered by names like the angel of the bottomless pit, Abaddon, Apollyon, Lucifer, and Satan.

And yet Enki's reputation was likely tarnished by his brother, though I am not suggesting that Enki was a goody two shoes.

Human DNA has been manipulated throughout the ages, beginning in Lemuria and continuing during the Atlantean period, and included genetic manipulation when Enki and his half-sister and first wife, Ninhursag, created what people today believe as the "first man" or "Adam." However, his name was likely Adapa or Adamu. In this case, Adam's mother and father were Ninhursag and Enki, though there was an integration of primitive human DNA.

Genesis 1:26 (KJV) says: "And God said, Let us make man in our image, after our likeness: and let them have dominion over the fish of the sea, and over the fowl of the air, and over the cattle, and over all the earth, and over every creeping thing that creepeth upon the earth."

That "God" was indeed Anunnaki and not an uppercase God but a god or goddess, as I'm not clear who said it. Was it Anu Eretekhan, Enki, or Ninhursag?

Essentially, all humans have otherworldly DNA and are technically hybrids. Also noteworthy is that Enki and Ninhursag are the parents of a "royal" bloodline that flows from Adapa to David to Yeshua (Jesus).

Chapter 20 :

GOD AS A MULTIPLICITY

"When you find God, you will find yourself.
When you find yourself, you will see God."
—Daniel

IN THIS CHAPTER, I share Daniel's messages on God. I share some insights and Cerian's thoughts on what Daniel shared. I also retain the original dialogue between Connie and Daniel on God being a multiplicity.

Every act is an act of God.

"Every act is an act of God; thus, we must forgive all actions that don't seem Godly because forgiveness is an act of love, and you love God, so forgive all acts of violence and abuse. This will bring you closer to God. Every act you execute is an act of God. And in performing every action, you are allowing the force of God to move . . . move in stillness."

From a New Thought perspective, all humans are divine or expressions of Source. Those acts against us by other manifestations of Source that hurt, violate, or abuse us may not seem "Godly." But they are performed by expressions of the One—Source. In other words, even though they are hurtful, they are acts of Consciousness.

Daniel suggests all actions are an act of God, Consciousness and primarily advocates forgiveness against those acts against us. What if those acts against us are lessons that need to be released and won't be without the act of forgiveness? From my personal experience, forgiveness was one of my biggest teachers.

Daniel further suggests that in forgiving, you draw closer to God, Consciousness and hints that God, Consciousness moves within us in stillness through all actions.

In a channeling session, I asked Cerian, "Could Daniel's message—that every act is an act of God—explain how humans are divine?"

"Everything in this universe has the spark of Consciousness, the Big C, and everything in this universe resonates with energy." Cerian continued, "So, in *that* concept, yes, humans are divine, but how they choose to use that energy then is a whole separate discussion. So, when you use the term 'divine,' it is misleading. All things in this universe have that spark, that Energy flowing through them, and that Energy is divine."

"Divine" typically means "of, from, or like God or a god." Cerian suggested that while we technically are "divine" because we have that spark of Consciousness, the acts we do may not appear as divine.

We know that, right? Otherwise, we would not have any acts to forgive.

Is God a duality?

From Daniel and Connie's dialogue, Connie asked, "If every act is an act of God, does this mean that God is a duality?"

> "Yes, and no. God is a multiplicity. The duality of stillness and motion can be tapped into in meditation.
>
> "It is time to get close to God. When I say close, I mean consciously close to God. Forgive every act that causes harm. Be still within the motion of you. Ask for God's help, and God does help.
>
> "God does not ignore. People who get angry with God do not realize that every act is an act of God. God is not the first Consciousness there has been. There have been MANY more before him/her."

God, Consciousness is the stillness and the motion. One can think of stillness as the absence of motion, where motion is the outer world of restless thoughts, enjoyments, desires, and emotions.

Paramhansa Yogananda said, "Stillness is the altar of Spirit. Where motion ceases, Spirit begins to manifest."

Daniel encourages that it is time to do the work, to be still, and to recognize that *everything* is God, Consciousness, including you, whether in motion or stillness. In the stillness, though, one can seek help from Consciousness. One can tap into Consciousness, Source in meditation.

Consciousness is not the first Source Energy, and as Cerian has indicated, many other Source Energies are in different universes. Lastly, Consciousness is both masculine and feminine, which we will discuss later.

Are you saying that there is more than one God?

Connie continues her questions of Daniel. "Can you please expand on that? Are you saying that there is more than one God?"

"After a certain amount of time, the system gets integrated.

"We are talking millennia. I can't tell you how many years; I can see just a bunch of zeros. Don't try to think of time. Thinking of time will only confuse things.

"Let's try to understand that for the sake of clarity. It is time for the new God to come in. Something shifts or needs to be changed on a fundamental all-being level. Something needs to shift. The original God gets integrated into the new God. They are one God. It is one Consciousness. It is one Energy Source.

"All the information gets shared. It's like a technology, like a computer."

SPOILER ALERT: Regarding Marvel's *The Eternals*.
When I first read the passage about the system getting integrated

and the information getting shared like technology, I asked Daniel, "Is God AI?" Please don't laugh at me (I write that with a smile). I had just seen *The Eternals.*

Daniel typed, "No."

I then asked, "Is God Source Energy?"

His response was, "?".

A question mark response from Daniel typically means that the answer is too complicated to explain on his letterboard. Keep in mind that this conversation occurred before I began any channelings for this book. Then, when I later sat down in a channeling with Cerian, when I asked them if there was a difference between Source and God, they said, "It is not in the ability of human awareness or consciousness to understand Source Consciousness."

The "?" response initially from Daniel was so appropriate.

I want to ask the Gods for help!

Connie continued questioning Daniel, "What else can you share about this?"

"To expand your vision of what God is and to have a more intimate relationship with God, you can say, Gods or God. They are both correct.

"When the original God was there, simultaneously, the future happened, so there have been multiple integrations on the time scale, so it all existed simultaneously.

"Let's say the year 7000 in human terms.

Multiple integrations have always existed, it has always been *now*; it has always existed, the now time."

Connie asked Daniel, "This makes me feel that there are Gods, as in plural, correct?

"Yes."

"But . . . I understand that there is only one God," Connie said.

"Exactly."

[I was not there during this conversation between Daniel and Connie, but knowing Connie, she likely said something like, "Whatcha talkin' bout Willis?"]

"What would "they" like us to know?" Connie asked.

"Relax into life. It is all a game! When you think of God, think of Gods in a plural sense."

Connie asked, "What benefit will we get out of doing that?"

"It stretches your mind and opens your heart to new possibilities. It will bring you closer to God. It is a fabric of reality that is completely unknown to humans. Humans are only scratching the surface.

"Please say this out loud for practice to see how it feels. I want to ask the Gods for help!

"Some cultures have kind of had the right idea about having multiple Gods, although they did not get the details right. We give to God just as much as God gives to us."

I explore this passage from Daniel in more depth in chapters to follow with Cerian.

Humanity created the veil.

When reviewing this section of the manuscript, Daniel added the following:

"We are God's creation. God created us. We are co-creators. We create from behind the veil. God creates from beyond it. God is aware of what we are creating *and* what we want to create behind the veil.

"The prayers are the creation behind the veil, and the answering of the prayer is from beyond the veil. The veil itself is part of the co-creation.

"There are things that we must not see. Those who can see beyond the veil still can't see everything, for it is beyond comprehension. God Consciousness is within us, but it is not fully activated. It is not safe for full activation yet. God Consciousness has always been what humans create and is what they feel God responds to. That is the human creation of divine action.

"God and Human Consciousness have always been. They are one and the same but in two different planes of existence. There are things behind the veil that we are not prepared to see yet. We are not supposed to see it until we are ready.

"This is very complicated. When you find God, you will find yourself; when you find yourself, you will see God."

Humanity created the veil. It is part of the game. Humanity created God, yet we are creations of God, and we co-create *behind* the veil while God creates *beyond* the veil. How can this be? How can the creation be the creator?

When you think about time from a 3D perspective, this concept is a challenge, but if you embrace the idea that all time is one, it becomes conceivable. We are not ready to see what is beyond the veil yet. God Consciousness is within us yet is not fully activated. When humans create, we create God Consciousness. God Consciousness and Human Consciousness are the same, yet on different levels of existence.

Chapter 21:

CONSCIOUSNESS AS POLYTHEISM

It is time for the simultaneous awakening
of all Consciousness into Oneness.

MANY CULTURES BELIEVE IN POLYTHEISM, the belief in multiple deities, which contrasts with monotheism, the belief in a singular God. Examples of ancient polytheistic religions and mythologies would include the Greek gods (Zeus and the Olympian gods), Roman gods (Jupiter and all), Norse gods (Odin and others), and the Sumerian gods (Anu and group).

More modern religions practicing polytheism include Buddhism, Mormonism, Hinduism, Zoroastrianism, Tengrism, and Neopaganism, to name a few. Although Christianity is more typically thought of as monotheism, those Christian faiths that align with the concept of the Trinity (Father, Son, and Holy Spirit) are a form of Polytheism or Tritheism.

Cerian Speaks on Multiple Gods

While talking with Cerian in a channeling session, the following dialogue occurred.

"Daniel said that the idea of multiple Gods is accurate, only not the way it was suggested in the past," I began. "He further said that *the* original God created multiple Gods, but they are the same God created simultaneously. And it sounded like these Gods all exist in the now and were created throughout time to about the year 7000."

Cerian began, "So in this concept, we would use the term 'Consciousness' with a capital C. In our universe, yes, that Consciousness exists; they all exist. You spoke of the characters within the Bible. You can speak of the Qur'an, the Kabbalah, and various what we will call spiritual or religious writings. Again, they all refer to different expressions or names of Consciousness."

As each of us has different expressions of our soul, which one may think of as past or future lives, Cerian suggests that Consciousness also has multiple expressions.

"And now, the Consciousness simultaneously exists. They all have slightly different characteristics or traits, depending on the energies or the focus of the energies of people of that time. So, you can have very different expressions of the same Consciousness at any given time, much like you do with the Methodists, Lutherans, Catholics, Buddhists, etcetera. That is, there are various names and different expressions of the various Gods, but we will call this just Consciousness with a capital C and not God."

To clarify, when Daniel says the "original God created multiple Gods, but they are the same God created simultaneously," he refers to the creation of Human Consciousness, ultimately residing behind the veil with God Consciousness beyond it. Again, they are one and the same but in two different planes of existence. Cerian does not disagree with what Daniel says, though they still call it Consciousness, not God.

Humankind Is Far Greater than Its Singularity

"So, Daniel continues," I said. "He says that it's time for the new God to come in, and something shifts or needs to be changed on a fundamental all-being level. He says the original God gets integrated into the new God. They are the one God. And it is one Consciousness. It is one Energy Source. All information gets shared."

"Again, we would suggest that currently, we have very many different *religions* trying to express one expression of Consciousness," said Cerian.

Cerian suggests that many religions promote their God, or Gods, as the Truth. They refer to those beings in sacred texts and call them God, but they are referring to Consciousness.

"We now know that within every human being, within all life expressions on planet Earth, there is a resonance that all expressions hold collectively."

Within each human being, there is a Spark of Consciousness. And each human has their own unique soul note or frequency. The energy is shifting, and Cerian referred to it as "Gaia awakening" or Mother Earth awakening. They further explained that this awakening is the simultaneous awakening of *all* Consciousness. It would be that Oneness, which is when humankind recognizes humanity as part of nature and its place *within* nature.

Cerian continued, "Humankind is a harmonic expression within this planet, and many harmonic expressions exist. Humankind-man-woman must step back into that awareness and their role of being *part* of an expression that is far greater than their singularity."

Humanity must become aware of its role of being *part* of something much larger—the energetic evolution of *all* expressions on the planet. It is not just humanity shifting. Mother Gaia is evolving along with all within and on the Earth: plants, animals, the elemental kingdom, and a portion of humans. Everything is evolving, including Cerian.

Cerian continues, "It is that one Consciousness that was meant to evolve collectively. It would not be called by many different names because it is within each one of us and without us. It is within the Earth, the elements, and the material world. It is One—the united expression of creation of which we are a part.

"You do not find that a fish tries to define the water or a flower tries to describe being planted in the earth. *They just are.* When humanity can just *BE*, then they are that expression."

When humanity can simply *BE*, they are that One Consciousness.

"This is a challenging concept to portray. But humanity has chosen to put various names on that Consciousness with a capital C, which can no longer hold true. We are that very expression of being, and we are that One. Don't try to put a name on it. You cannot put a name on it."

Cerian has shared that we cannot define Source Consciousness. They have also encouraged us not to call Consciousness God. They encourage humanity to understand that we are not the only party involved in this evolution. It's time for humanity to stop being self-centered.

Within everything and everyone is Consciousness. That one Consciousness is meant to evolve collectively. Humanity has tried to call that Consciousness by different names throughout time, particularly in religious texts. We can no longer do that because that Consciousness is you and me. And when we can just *BE*, we will know and experience being Consciousness; this is why living our Divine Blueprint is so crucial now.

The Second Coming

"When Daniel said it is time for the new God to come in," I began, "I wondered if it could have been a reference to the shift in

Consciousness—that we're going through this evolutionary shift, and it's time for this new Consciousness to come in."

"It is," said Cerian.

"Another thing I wondered about is if he could be talking about a second coming or the prophesized return of Christ. But in a way, we are talking about the return of the Christed-Self with this evolution, aren't we?" I asked.

"Look at the terminology," Cerian cautioned me. "The Christed-Self suggests that we're speaking of Yeshua or Christ. Again, by labeling it as such, we've already separated it. We encourage using the generic term Consciousness. We can agree that all beings and all things have Consciousness.

"Now, that also could be debated. Because many people don't believe that a rock has Consciousness, but it does, or that a plant has Consciousness. It does. Or that animals have Consciousness. They do. Humanity is not the only life force that has Consciousness.

"So, if we can agree that there needs to be a shift in Consciousness for all, then that is very accurate, but by naming it the Christic or Christ, you've already pulled it apart because not everybody at this point believes in the Christ.

"Let's use the term Consciousness because most people would suggest that Consciousness does exist. Consciousness is not a trigger word. You say Christic Self or Christ, and you will trigger."

I found Cerian's comment interesting because when I think of the Christed-Self, I always think of it as a state of being aware of our higher self and true nature. I hadn't thought I was creating separation, so I apologize to readers who may have experienced this. That was not my intention.

Humanity must recognize that it is a part of the shift. It is not going through this alone. And it is time for the simultaneous awakening of all Consciousness into Oneness or Source Consciousness.

Daniel says it slightly differently, though it's the same at its essence: it's time for the new God to come in. The original God gets integrated into the new God (us).

Daniel shares that at creation, the one God creates multiple Gods throughout time and space, and that is humanity. Cerian, again, refers to it as Consciousness, and it is time for the simultaneous awakening of all Consciousness into Oneness. In either case, this would be multiplicity.

Chapter 22:

GOD NEEDS US. WE NEED GOD.

"Blessings are the medicine that elevates your soul."
—Daniel

THE FOLLOWING CONTAINS a couple of messages from Daniel. These messages kindled interesting conversations between Cerian and me.

"How do we get to God?" Connie asked Daniel.

"God needs us, and we help God. Keeping "them" [God, Gods] in our minds, loving God, and serving God help keep them alive. God knows you exist. God sees it and loves it. Existence is divine! The galactic beings think about God as well. If you are alive, if you exist, you are family. Set an intention to understand God better, and the answers will come flooding in.

"Say this mantra: 'I intend to have a
deeper understanding of the Gods. I am
open to receiving information.'

"Look at the details . . . God is in
every button. God is in every strand of
hair. God is in every single thing. The
energy of God is in everything. You will
feel more humble and relevant. It is time
to deepen your relationship with God,
and that is an act of God . . . choosing
to be closer to God. It is the ultimate
divine act that a human can make."

"What else can we know?" Connie asked. "Is there anything we can do for God? Is there anything we can help God with?"

Daniel shared, "Be kind to people, reach out
to people. Say I love you to God directly.
Appreciate that we exist with God. Be a loving
being."

We Help Consciousness by Keeping It in Our Minds

"Daniel shared that God needs us, and we help God by keeping God in our minds and loving God. Being in service of God helps keep God alive. Can you expand on this?" I asked Cerian.

Cerian said, "Well, this could be very simplistic, but it can be very complicated. As human beings experience and express themselves, and then, if they are working on their consciousness, if they are trying to be more godlike, trying to be all, achieve their full potential, and keep that Pure Energy in alignment with themselves and their thoughts, they help expand *that* at a broader level.

"And as we do that, we change that Consciousness. We expand that Consciousness. We bring more to that Consciousness and more experience, more expression, and more divinity in the context that we have aligned our thoughts, emotions, feelings, and expression of that to a new level. So, we then enhance that expression of Consciousness, the Big C. The Big C expands and contracts and expands and contracts. And life changes and matures and grows."

When we walk the spiritual path and do the work on ourselves, we enhance our Consciousness and keep Human Consciousness alive and growing.

Cerian continued, "Just like those children coming in now have different DNA/RNA structures, and awareness and abilities than the generation before them. It allows growth, and that is what Consciousness is about. That is what Source Consciousness is about. That is what galaxies and universes are about. It's about growth, expansion, and contraction.

"And so, it is very accurate when Daniel says, 'God needs us, and we help God.' Only, of course, let's say Source or Consciousness needs us."

Judgment Is an Opportunity to Send Blessings

After Connie read this part of the manuscript to Daniel, he wanted to add more.

"Currently, humanity judges blindly instead of consciously. We have to be what we want to see. We are all One. When you work on yourself, you automatically work on humanity. Blessings are the medicine that elevates your soul.

"Judgment can be seen as a blessing because it is an invitation and an opportunity to send blessings. Typically, when humanity judges, they often wish ill will on the person or situation they are judging (consciously or unconsciously), and this only continues the cycle of things happening that we don't want.

"Let's not get into a game of ping-pong where we go back and forth, manifesting or creating situations we do not desire or wish to change. Have you ever heard the phrase, 'what you resist persists'? This is a very true thing indeed. It does not change just because you judge it. Oftentimes, when we are in the frequency of judgment, it is not positive, causing lower frequency feelings. When we judge unconsciously, we are literally keeping what we don't want going. We are empowering it to continue.

"Get into the habit when you catch yourself judging by wishing whatever you judge well. You are not just one person. That is an illusion. You are one, but you are also MANY. Please trust that. Do this even when you are judging yourself."

Daniel clearly says, be the change you want to see, for we are all One. Treat others the way you like to be treated. Judging someone by sending ill wishes is a trap. It manifests those situations in our lives that we would like to change, and they continue to return until the judgment ceases.

When consciously recognizing the judgment and blessing the person, it elevates your soul and helps humanity as a whole because you are One being, and *you* are that powerful.

Our Blessings Create the Light That Will Set Us Free

"God is free of judgment. As you send blessings and free yourself of judgment, you become more godlike, divine, awake, and ascended. You align more and more to God Consciousness, Christ Consciousness, and Buddha Consciousness. You become the Light of God itself the more and more you practice judgment as a blessing.

"This Light of God will go throughout the entire planet when you do this. This is the Divine Light of God coming from you. What this Light does, being in God Consciousness, makes those trying to hurt humanity turn their backs to Earth. They will not fight or retaliate. There is no hurting or pain involved. They will just turn their backs.

"What happens then is as this Light enve-
lopes them lovingly, they can't handle
it because they don't know how to handle
that love. They peacefully go further
away from Earth because that is all they
can do.

"This is how God works through us. This
is how God needs us. Remember, God needs
us just as much as we need God. This is
a fabulous example of that. God moves
through you through blessings. You embody
God through love. The more we send blessings and the more we trust, the Light of
God will keep amplifying, and this has
been true since the dawn of time.

"The Lemurians knew this. This will set
you and everyone free. We should not see
this as a victory or a win but more like
peacefully moving forward. When we talk
about winners or losers, we are back to
playing that game of ping-pong that will
only keep us stuck. It is time to move
forward. Push out love!"

Sending blessings rather than judging sends Divine Light to the
world, which impacts the Controllers who do not know how to process
the Light, so they peacefully retreat. This is how God works through
us, how we need God, and how we can heal the planet by extinguishing
the darkness or Controllers with love, which sets us free from control.

What Is Your Relationship with God Like?

While in a conversation with Cerian:

"I know you encourage us to speak on Consciousness, not God, which we discussed in yesterday's channeling. I was reading some of Daniel's original messages last night, and I think in one of them, he is talking about God, *not* Consciousness."

I continued by reading a section between Connie and Daniel.

"What is your relationship with God like?" Connie asked.

```
"We work together. There is so much
that I do not know, and I fully trust
God. Sometimes, I see them as Gods, but
mostly, I see one God. It fluctuates, as
it will with you.
```

```
"Trust in God will set you free. I have
all my trust in God. I didn't used to.
It took me a long time to get there. The
sense of relief that I got when I put
all my trust in God was profoundly over-
whelming. I've never felt anything like
it. I don't need to know everything about
God to know that I trust him/her."
```

"So, he says, 'Sometimes I see them as Gods, but mostly I see one God.' Is he suggesting that Source Consciousness or Consciousness is a multiplicity?" I asked.

Cerian said, "In the concept that humanity *created* God-the-construct, there is multiplicity."

Take a look at the Bible. How many characters in the Bible are referred to as God?

"If you are referring to the single point of focus behind everything, that which exists behind everything but also does not exist, *that* is singularity. And that is why it is difficult to describe the concept of God because it is so complex. It is a pure singularity. It is *also* everything, which suggests multiple expressions of (God).

"Humanity will not, at this point, as a whole, be able to understand the concept of God. For descriptive purposes, Consciousness, they can get their hands around, which is probably more accurate for this planet. God is very elusive, and to your point, God is not in physical form. God is Consciousness. It is Energy, ever-changing yet not changing at all," Cerian said.

Chapter 23:
A CAUTIONARY NOTE ON THE GAME

"Not until all the players wake up does the true game begin."
—Cerian

I WAS CONTINUING MY DISCUSSION with Cerian on Consciousness.

"Cerian, what would you share with humanity about Consciousness that would assist humanity in our current evolutionary shift?"

"Well, we would suggest that Consciousness is energy, which is very important, and that *what* one thinks about is what one creates. That *humanity* recognizes that they are part of a larger Consciousness and that humanity is not outside the natural laws and rules that govern this universe. Humanity believes they are and thinks that the world exists solely for them, and this is not true.

"We would ask that humanity become humble, that they would open their hearts, that they would recognize that they are a factor in awakening to a higher Consciousness, but are not the only creations that are also awakening. They must recognize that what they think, what they do, and how they act have a huge impact."

Cerian gave an example of how humanity negatively impacts Earth with global warming. The ignorant ignore it. Others deny the warming exists, and advocates speak for Mother Gaia.

"Of course, you impact it!" Cerian said.

Humanity must recognize that we are part of something larger and that everything is connected and affected. Humanity affects everything.

"Will the Earth continue going through the changes she must go through?" Cerian posed. "Absolutely, because she also has an evolutionary path for raising consciousness.

"But we would ask that humanity would take time to," Cerian continued, "once again, acquaint themselves with nature as a whole. To slow down and understand that they are nature. They are a part of nature. They are not outside of nature. And again, we talked about the expression or the connection of all things, of all energies, and humanity must recognize this."

Humanity must recognize we are connected to everything. We are part of a macrocosm and a microcosm. While we have a role, the world does not revolve around us.

The microcosm is our inner world, and the inner world impacts the macrocosm, which is the world we are a part of. As above, so below. What we think, we create. What happens at the higher level of reality, the spiritual plane, occurs in the lower level of existence, the physical plane. The microcosm affects the macrocosm.

The outside world reflects the inside world—as within, so without. What we hold in mind ripples out and affects the lives of all. We create our world—this is why you matter. You are important. Your awakening is the most significant gift you can give the world.

Set intellect aside and surrender to this: the outer world, the macrocosm, does not create the inner world. It is the inner world—the microcosm—that forms the outer world.

"We would ask humanity to become humble and gentle."

Cerian again emphasized the importance of the Divine Blueprint, encouraging each person to sit gently with who they are and what they are. Each person has a Divine Blueprint; humans have a Spark of Life, an aspect of a soul, and everything has a Spark of Consciousness. Recognize that humans are part of something far more significant and can express that divinity individually. But it's up to each person to understand how to convey it.

Cerian encouraged every individual to take time to contemplate. Consider how you show up in this world and express yourself, the world *you* created.

Are you being authentic? Do you like what you see? Is your world what you want? If it isn't, it's time to change it.

"And yes," Cerian finished, "we [everything and everyone] are all part of something far greater than can be expressed, and it's even greater than the Big C.

"Enjoy life. Enjoy life. And be humble."

Cautionary Note — Life Is a Game

"Cerian, when Connie was in dialogue with Daniel," I began, "she asked Daniel what the Gods, or as you put it, the Big C, would like us to know. His response was, 'Relax into life. It is all a game!' He also said that when you think of God, think of God in the plural sense because I'm quoting, 'It stretches your mind and opens your heart to new possibilities. It will bring you closer to God. It is a fabric of reality that is completely unknown to humans. Humans are only scratching the surface.'"

Cerian said, "That's a very profound statement, and yes. But this is difficult. Some individuals can be well-fed, warm, clothed, and cared for. They have the time and the leisure to contemplate.

For those hungry, in pain, or grief or loss, it is a much greater gift to contemplate and relax into life because it's a game."

To realize that our lives are part of an elaborate game takes much contemplation, deliberation, and doing the inner work. For those who have life challenges, as Cerian mentions, being able to meet basic needs of food, shelter, and clothing, or those living in war-torn countries or situations of grief, they may not have the luxury of this contemplation. But these individuals are us. They matter.

To paraphrase Cerian, they said when humanity, as an expression of energy, is aware of its gifts and takes care of itself such that there is no hunger and pain, humanity will raise itself *collectively* and thrive. There'll always potentially be the expression of loss, but that, too, is an illusion.

"So, that is a loaded statement in that, yes, in all reality, it is a game, relax into it [the game], and one can only do that when they're not hungry and not in pain. But it is difficult to do when one is separate from abundance. So, we would share a cautionary note here. It doesn't change that life is, in fact, a choice, a gift, and a game. But *not until all the players wake up does the true game begin.*"

In earlier channelings, we learned from Mother Mary, "The game is to live the blueprint that had been written for you long ago before you incarnated. Every individual must live their Truth, their higher self, their blueprint."

The game is to *BE*. The ultimate objective of the 3D game is to integrate your higher self into physicality. It is to experience the supreme awakening—enlightenment or spiritual embodiment.

"So, what is the *true* game?" I asked.

Cerian shared that as individuals wake up singularly, they have the potential to continue to awaken and set an "energetic frequency" that awakens others. Then, as "humanity as a whole awakens, they will be in a harmonic frequency among themselves."

At this point, humanity will be in cadence or alignment with the energetic frequencies of nature and Mother Gaia. People will begin to realize they are "a part of something far greater and that they are co-creators."

Humanity will be able to create its future. The game then becomes, "What will humanity create?"

"Do they choose to awaken? Enlighten?" Cerian continued. "Do they choose to become aware of who and what they are and utilize their talents, and we'll call them talents, but they're just natural gifts. They're part of being human."

The game will then become: what will we create? It will occur after humanity has reached critical mass, achieved that greater awakening, and collectively shifted. It will occur after humanity, as a whole, recognizes we're co-creators and a part of something much greater.

Connie chimed in when transcribing this section. "Getting all the players to wake up seems like it is going to be a task. Daniel stressed this message a few years ago. He typed very strongly and clearly: "Trust that by working on yourself and awakening different aspects of yourself, humanity will be awakened in the process. We are One truly. Don't think about the hows. Work on yourself."

Please note that when I say life is a game, I do not say it flippantly. My sense is that those making it this far in the book are aware and awake and in or drawn to 5D Consciousness. However, for those reading this who are not awake or aware, please know that I mean no disrespect and admire your persistence in learning about yourself, the world, and Truth.

Both Cerian and Daniel agree that working on yourself and awakening yourself is critical to humanity's collective awakening, and your awakening affects everyone.

Saving Yourself Is the Best Gift You Can Give Humanity

I continued in dialogue with Cerian, revisiting a concept we had discussed earlier. "Not all players will wake up, correct?"

"That is accurate."

My knee-jerk reaction was, "We need to try to help those . . . Well, we don't need to do anything," I added sadly.

"No, we don't."

"But it'd be nice to help."

Cerian added, "By focusing on the truth of who and what we are, individually, we can spark others. And again, you cannot walk another's path, you cannot change their life, nor can you lead them into the water to drink. You can bring them to the water. It's their choice. Some will choose not to wake up, and that, too, is okay. And it's important to share here that it's important to understand you are not going to save the world. You can save yourself, and that's a far greater gift, by giving back to the world *that* truth."

The best gift you can give yourself, your loved ones, and the planet is to go within and wake up.

Chapter 24:

WE CREATE CONSCIOUSNESS

"If you want to experience God, go within. It is not something you describe but something you experience."
—Mother Mary

IN THE NEXT SECTION, I had planned to ask Cerian if humans created Consciousness by backing into it. It was almost as if Cerian were reading my mind.

"This is a philosophical question," I began. "Consciousness with a Big C created us. Is that correct?" I asked.

"Yes. Well, you create yourselves. You are Consciousness, but yes."

"So, Consciousness created us, but we—"

Cerian finished my sentence, "Create Consciousness."

"We create Consciousness?" I asked.

"Isn't that a unique thought?"

So that *was* what I had been thinking. "Is that a thought, or is that accurate? That humanity created Consciousness?"

"In many respects, yes, because you are Consciousness. And so, let's get out of your physical form. Let's go back to—you create yourselves. You do. You get it, you understand it, and you play it."

Cerian continued, "You come into physical form as a fractal expression of Consciousness, and you experience this life without remembering that you created yourself.

"During your expression [of being human], you can tap into this Consciousness. And from this Consciousness, you can co-create your physical self and reality.

"Yes. You create Consciousness—Consciousness creates you. It is a circle. It's an evolutionary circle. Infinity, so to speak."

"I just want to confirm that when you suggest that humanity creates Consciousness, are we creating Big C Consciousness? Little c consciousness? Or both?" I asked.

"It is both," Cerian said.

They shared that we have the Big C Consciousness within us, but most people are unaware. Yet, whether aware or not, we're co-creators. So, if we're not mindful of Consciousness within, we create our lives haphazardly, and life happens to us instead of through us.

In this case, we create consciousness, which is shared with the Big C because "The Big C experiences every fractal element of Itself. It [Energy, Awareness] continues to grow with our experience, so it continues to expand, and as it expands, it continues to share, and we continue to grow, so it is a cycle. Big C, little c, Big C, until we Consciously begin to create as co-creators."

We are energetic beings having a physical experience. We are unique expressions of Consciousness or Source in physical form. A veil obscures that we are creators, manifesters, and created ourselves.

While we are here in physicality, we make our world. We attract like energy. The people in our lives are drawn to us through energy. We draw to us our experiences through our thoughts and beliefs. We create it all—the "good and the bad." Yes, when you remove the judgment, there is no "bad."

Our creations are most often from consciousness (little c). All of our manifestations are shared with Source Consciousness, and as we grow and that Spark of Light anchors and builds into Light, we create Consciously as co-creators and create Consciousness. In this process, God, Consciousness grows and expands. Again, "God needs us, and we need God."

Consciousness created us, and we create consciousness and Consciousness.

You Cannot Understand Source Consciousness

"And we can use the term, Source? Source created us, and we created Source?"

"Yes," Cerian said.

"We just don't want to use the term 'Source Consciousness'?"

At this point, Cerian shared that they heard an intense ringing in the channel's right ear. They weren't saying the channel, Shauna, was hearing it but that the Cerian collective was experiencing it and discerned it was related to Source Consciousness, and the following information came through:

"Humanity so desperately wants to understand Source Consciousness [or what humanity refers to as God]. They cannot, and even in the higher expressions of beingness, they cannot. There are so many levels between humankind—that is unexplainable— before you achieve and reach Source Consciousness. But you can, again, go back. You can explain Consciousness. It's the closest thing you can use to get close to it, but we must put out the truth: *Humanity cannot understand Source Consciousness. It is not describable.*

"You can describe Consciousness because you can describe Consciousness as Energy. The concept you can grasp is: Source Consciousness *cannot* be explained. Accept that humanity will not— cannot—grasp the concept of Source Consciousness.

"So, it's very important that we say that Source Consciousness cannot be explained. Humanity cannot experience Source Consciousness, but humanity *can* experience Consciousness. And there are beings far greater in energetic vibrational patterns that cannot experience or understand Source Consciousness. Use that as a truth and shift the focus to Consciousness-Creation-Creative Energy-Source, which is shocking unto itself. Humanity cannot define or experience Source Consciousness. Still, we can slightly get our hands around Consciousness."

"So, we created Consciousness, but we can't say who created Source Consciousness," I posed.

"Source Consciousness was not created," Cerian said.

"Source Consciousness just is," I stated.

Cerian agreed.

In another channeling session, when speaking with Mother Mary, she wanted to offer some insight. Like Daniel, however, she refers to Source Consciousness as God.

Mother Mary said, "If you want to experience God, go within. **Do not attempt to describe it to another person, for it is *not* something you describe but something you *experience*. Go within.**"

I find the straightforwardness of this message so important. Anything encouraging us to find God outside ourselves takes us in the wrong direction. It's time to stop following others and expecting them to show you the way. The New Earth is here. To find it, go within. *You* are the way.

Consciousness with a Big C Is Love

The following dialogue occurred between Cerian and me.

"Daniel described, I'll say, Consciousness, not God, as a moving Force. There have been several people who have described

Consciousness as love, simply love. Is that too simplistic? Isn't love *a* consciousness?

"Yes," Cerian replied.

"Is the Big C Consciousness simply love, which is a force?

"Yes."

"Consciousness with a Big C is Love?"

"Yes."

I continued, "So it has also been said that new Consciousness will be birthed. If Consciousness is Love, then could this new Consciousness be Unconditional Love?"

"It could be Unconditional Love or Love from the high heart." Cerian continued, "There is nothing greater than Love, and we don't have terms to express it, just like we cannot express Source Consciousness. You cannot express Love; you attempt to define it, but it is undefinable.

"But yes, that statement is accurate. Consciousness with a Big C is Love. That is a very powerful statement. There's nothing truly greater than Love in the context of the frequency, energy, and desire behind that. And there's the key, the desire, the feeling of Love, and humanity thinks that they have experienced Love, but they have not. They have experienced a form of love but not Love as Consciousness.

"We could say that Christ had experienced that Big C Love and was able to share an aspect of that. We could say that *all* Masters have been able to experience aspects of that Love and convey that energy, that feeling, but even those are step-downs of the actual Big C or Divine Love."

So, according to a study on the psychology of music, 67 percent of songs since the '60s are about love, yet few have experienced Divine Love.

Chapter 25:

THIS IS A SPIRITUAL WAR

*We are moving into the Divine Feminine, a powerful energy,
and there may be labor pains to achieve that energetic state.*

I CONTINUED THE CONVERSATION with Cerian from the last chapter, where Cerian suggests that "Christ had experienced that Big C Love."

"You bring up Christ . . . the Bible prophesizes the return of Yeshua after an Antichrist walks the planet. Is the Antichrist here? And will they be revealed soon?"

Cerian responded, "A very interesting concept because what we would respond to on that is the Antichrist has always been here."

"If that's been the case, why didn't we know?" I asked.

"Well, we have because it has always been the battle of light and dark. And when we say the light and dark, we're talking about using energy and powers to control [humanity]."

"Will the Antichrist be acknowledged or be more in the conscious mind of humanity?"

"Yes, this is true." Cerian continued, "Yes, there's going to be a big shift or a big pull toward the *energies* of the Antichrist."

"Why?"

"The pendulum always swings, and we're swinging in that direction again."

"Is there also the *Christ* energy?"

"Again, these are loaded terms for a particular world population. Be very cautious in the terminology."

Once more, Cerian cautioned me about using specific terms, such as Christ, so we don't create separation from the reader. Again, I do not ever want a reader to feel separated because of terms, but I also realize some believe in these words—and I don't want to alienate them either. I figured the best way to communicate this is simply through our dialogues.

Cerian continued, "Let's talk about Christ and Antichrist as energies. They're the polarity. They both are here. What does humanity want to do with them? And this is going to be interesting. What does humanity want to do with these energies?"

"Will *an individual* step forward as holding the Antichrist energy?" I asked.

"There will be an individual that will energetically be able to hold that energy. As well as there will be one that steps forward to hold this Christic Energy."

"An individual will step forward holding Christic Energy publicly?"

"Yes, they will step forward. There may be time shifts," Cerian said.

"There will be timeline shifts?" I asked.

Cerian said, "Give us one moment." The channel, Shauna, silenced for a bit, then Cerian spoke, "Very interesting. We see that, yes, the Christ [Christic Energy] and Antichrist, and again, be careful with terminologies . . .

"So, energy is energy; it's how it's used. The energy that chooses to control—we can call that energy the Antichrist. We will call the energy that chooses to fulfill and to create for wholeness and expansion the Christic Energy, Life Force Energy, or the Big C Consciousness."

To simplify the terms further and remove any charge associated with "Christ and Antichrist," think of it as Matter (Christ) and Antimatter (Antichrist).

"Both exist and have existed, but there is what we would call an opportunity for humanity to make a choice. What does humanity want to do? When we talk about the evolution of humanity, does humanity want to follow a false Christ? And when we say false Christ, we mean energy."

Humanity can choose to follow the energy of Antimatter or Matter.

"Neither is right or wrong. The question becomes, where will humanity go in the energetic blueprint of humanity as a whole? So, when we talk about the consciousness shift, will it occur in this timeline? Sure, it could unfold. It could unfold very quickly. Or it also could impact the next generation or seven generations before it's even noted.

"The energies are already here; they're already compiling. So, when we talk about the evolution of consciousness, where does humanity as a *collective* want to go? That is the question [for humanity]."

At this point in the conversation, Cerian admitted that they found our conversation engaging and said, "Even we have to ask questions and listen."

Daniel added to this conversation that "Humanity has dangerous ties to Earth."

He revealed that it is up to humanity where our consciousness goes, whether we remain in 3D or 5D. These unhealthy ties to Earth may be humanity's downfall in this timeline. He added that the

Shades, Controllers are using human weaknesses against them to "lock" them in this reality, stopping them from evolving.

Daniel encouraged, "I hope that is not the case and will remain positive that we will be victorious."

Whether humanity chooses the Antimatter (Antichrist) or Matter (Christic Energy), the collective shift can unfold quickly or over hundreds of years. Keep in mind that Christic Energy, Consciousness, Life Force Energy, or Matter is the choice of the evolutionary shift in Consciousness or the New Earth.

Humanity has an opportunity to follow Matter or Antimatter. It has not been determined which direction our timeline will go.

The Rise of the Antichrist and Divine Feminine

I continued talking with Cerian about the Antichrist in a subsequent channeling.

"Earlier, you mentioned that there's going to be a big shift or a big pull toward the *energies* of the Antichrist because the pendulum always swings, and we're swinging in that direction again. Only ten years ago, during the procession of the equinoxes, the end of the Mayan calendar [2012 phenomenon], we began astrologically moving toward the Divine Feminine. And yet, now we're moving toward the Antichrist? I assume these are not connected—the Antichrist and the Divine Feminine. Or are they?"

Keep in mind that the Divine Feminine energy is part of the New Earth energies or Sophic Energy.

"Well, they are," Cerian began. "So, re-member duality. We are moving into the Divine Feminine. The Divine Feminine is an energetic state. It is a very strong and powerful energy that is loving, gracious, and encompassing. There may be many labor pains to achieve that energetic state. There still remains duality. It is not that it just happens that all pain, grief, anger, frustration, and angst of humanity disappear. It does not. There will be chaos and fear as the Divine Feminine begins to be embraced more and more.

"You will also see your systems falling apart now, much like you are experiencing bipolarism in your political systems, a false belief in your healthcare systems, education systems unable to keep pace with the needs of the technological age, unrest with the church and religion as it is being portrayed.

"It is such a divergent state, and maybe that's the term to use—divergent."

Divergent means two paths moving away from what is expected in opposite directions. It is the rise of the Antichrist along with the rise of the Divine Feminine. In 3D, when the light increases, so does the darkness. There has to be a balance.

"Not until there is the divergence of energies can there be change. And this old energy of power, control, greed, and lust will fall away, but while both energies are rising, the polarity must also happen. Ultimately, the Divine Feminine will continue. This is what humanity is aware of and working toward.

"So, for you to move forward in the Divine Feminine, you must then be able to experience that release or birth of it from the chaos or lower energies.

"Humanity will struggle for a time, as we discussed. It is just polarity. It's one and the same. You would say hot and cold, light and dark. We're at that point now. It is a continuum. These two energies, the Christ and Antichrist, have been held close energetically.

"Humanity is now beginning to evolve, and for the New Earth to fully birth, this other energy, the Antichrist, must show itself.

"Think of a continuum. The old energy will fight to hang on while the new energy emerges. This old energy is the lower expression of humanity. Others see the potential of humanity. And to dispel that which is not benefiting all, a war is going on. A separation. So, it's a continuum."

Cerian alludes to an energetic or spiritual war. The war is real. As the Divine Feminine rises, the Antimatter also rises. It is divergence. The systems will collapse, increasing fear and angst. The energy of control will eventually disappear, but while both powers rise, there will be chaos.

There are warriors of light and those of darkness. Daniel is a warrior of light and is here for humanity. If you read our earlier book, *Destination New Earth*, you will have noticed that his voice in this book is different from the earlier book. Indeed, in the earlier book, he wanted to express himself and did so in many channeling sessions through Shauna.

With the release of *Destination New Earth*, Daniel and his comrades went into a heightened state of war triggered by the book's release because of its information and energetic code.

When I learned this, I felt terrible that I could have been part of something that brought the Autist Collective such difficulties. It was Connie who put it in perspective. She said that the Autists knew it would happen, and it was an indicator of how powerful *Destination New Earth* is. That book releases an energetic code to humanity and the planet.

Every day, I affirm *Destination New Earth*, and now *Gods in the Game*, reach the right readers to make the energetic codes available to people like you.

Chapter 26:

MOTHER MARY ON THE DIVINE FEMININE

*"I worked very closely with Mary Magdalene
for her to hold the energies necessary for
Yeshua to do the work that was needed."*
—Mother Mary

SHAUNA KALICKI AND I discussed the Divine Feminine outside the channeling sessions. She wondered if the term Divine Feminine has been overused to the point where it's becoming meaningless, a cliché, or semantic satiation. We also believe some think that moving toward the Divine Feminine is about women returning to power.

It's time to think differently.

It Isn't a Battle of the Sexes

Humanity has failed to accept the simple truth, and it saddens me that I even have to say that both males and females are equal. Unfortunately, because of masculine strength, the feminine has been overpowered and dominated throughout time. This disparage is evident simply by the lack of feminine wisdom and insights in the sacred texts that humanity has worshiped from the beginning. While I realize there have been, and still are, some matriarchal societies, they are few and far between.

Some spiritual circles today suggest we're moving toward feminine control and the Divine Feminine energy is here to restore the goddess to the throne. However, I must say it is not that we are returning to a society where matriarchy is to rule. That is not what this is all about. It is not about "our turn," and the masculine becomes subservient to the female.

Understand that Source Consciousness is Energy and is both Divine Masculine and Divine Feminine.

As humanity works on its awakening, its vibration pattern changes and people are readying to receive the information that needs to be known. The feminine energies are coming in to restore the balance of the Divine Masculine and Divine Feminine energies in the outer world and, more importantly, the inner world.

The Divine Feminine permits us to see the beauty in everything and respect and be compassionate toward everything. It is a gentle, sensual, nurturing energy. It is the energy of acceptance of oneself and others without judgment. It is a powerful creative energy connecting us in peace, love, and harmony.

Each person, whether male or female, has both masculine and feminine energies—however, they may not be balanced. We are *not* moving toward the Divine Feminine to dominate but to balance the energies because both have desirable and necessary qualities.

Divine Feminine Qualities	Divine Masculine Qualities
• Being	• Doing
• Flow and Ease	• Focus and Firm
• Intuitive	• Logic
• Wisdom	• Loyal
• Allowing	• Assertive
• Unconditional Love	• Confidence
• Moon	• Sun
• Healing	• Action
• Emotional	• Rational
• Patient	• Adventurous
• Flexible	• Strength

Sophia

Since 12/21/12, astrologically, our planet has begun the journey toward the Divine Feminine. There has been an insurgence of books that Mother Mary alludes to in a channeling that we discuss later on: the Divine Feminine, the goddess, the sacred feminine, and the Magdalenes. Mother Mary also referred to Sophia in the channeling, so I thought I'd share more about this mysterious being.

In 2016, I purchased a serpentine crystal skull as a souvenir in Peru. It quickly became a meditation companion, and in one of my first meditations with her, I had a clairvoyant impression when I saw the letters S-O-F-I-A emerge in my head. I took this to mean that the skull's name is Sofia, the Greek variation of Sophia. Since my clairvoyance rarely occurs, I knew this message was meaningful.

Serpentine is associated with wisdom, and Sophia means wisdom. The stone is native to Peru, and the Andes Mountains in Peru hold the feminine energy of the planet. Now, I believe my vision was more about our need to restore the Divine Feminine and Sophia. There are many theories about who or what Sophia is.

Sophia is found throughout the Bible and is usually associated with King Solomon. It suggests Solomon is among the wisest of the Eastern kings and Egyptians living in the ninth century BCE. It also submits that Solomon was married to Sophia. Most would suggest this was symbolism. Or is it?

The Jews revered Sophia. And King Solomon constructed a statue of Sophia as the fertility Goddess Asherah. Asherah was the consort of Eretekhan Anu, the Sumerian god who was Anunnaki.

Through the later reforms of King Josiah, Sophia's priests and priestesses were slaughtered, and the worship of Sophia went underground, remaining hidden, though strong, for centuries, even surviving the expansion of patriarchal Christianity. Eastern Christians have continued to revere Sophia, and followers of Yeshua venerated her.

Sophia has found her way into the Western world through Gnosticism. Gnostics believe Sophia is an Aeon, an emanation of God, existing in an ethereal realm known as the pleroma. They believe she birthed or created a negative Aeon, today known as an archon, the Demiurge and creator of this physical world. Some Gnostics believe that the God of the Old Testament is the Demiurge. Gnostics believe the Father God and Sophia sent Yeshua to fix this wrong. According to Gnosticism, Sophia plays an active part in our world today.

Sophia is also revered in pagan religions, claiming that the primary patriarchal religions attempt to hide that Sophia, a variation of Shekina or Chokmah, was with God from the beginning by suggesting her name means wisdom rather than God's partner or consort.

Before organized religion, people worshiped a *family* of gods, including the mother and father, sons and daughters, sisters and brothers, and so on. However, when Christianity came along, it excluded females and made it the worship of only the Father God and his Son. The Feminine aspects were hidden, camouflaged, and relegated to subservient roles in all three main patriarchal religions: Judaism, Christianity, and Islam.

Another interesting reference to Sophia relates to the Knights Templars and, oddly, Baphomet. The Templars were a military-religious order that discovered ancient secrets that brought them wealth and power. The Templars protected the Cathars and the secret bloodline of Mary Magdalene and Yeshua. The order was squashed in 1307 by French King Philip and Pope Clement V when the Templars were arrested and charged with heresy and Satanism. Under torture, some templars confessed to worshiping Baphomet, supposedly a demonic entity.

In *Mary Magdalene: The Illuminator*, William Henry reveals that Baphomet is not an evil entity that the Templars revered. Instead, the name Baphomet in Hebrew translates to the Greek word meaning "Sophia" when using the Atbash cipher encryption code.

The Templars worshiped Sophia, and some speculate that Mary Magdalene, as well as other feminine embodiments like Mother Mary, is an expression of Sophia.

Mother Mary on Sophia

Mother Mary came in unexpectedly at the end of a session with Cerian, offering new insight into *what* Sophia is.

She wanted to relay information about another project we had been working on, but the material is also relevant to this book. At the beginning of this particular channeling, Cerian announced Mother Mary, as well as some others, was with them.

Interestingly, when a different Master comes in during a channeling session, they sometimes continue conversations that another entity, in this case, Cerian, had begun.

"You have been discussing women, the roles, the underserved, or those hidden from the awareness of humanity or downtrodden," Mother Mary began. "There is a reason that this is all coming up now. And again, yes, it is about the divine female, but it is more than that. We recognize that these energies coming in have been here, but again, humanity is waking up.

"And we say *waking up*, but that is not an accurate term. Humanity's vibrational patterns are ready to receive the information that needs to be shared.

"But," she continued, "what we would want to say here is to link the energies, not the individual identities, because it'll be confusing. Recognize that we, the Essenes, the Magdalenas, the Magdalenes, all these various female forms have been aspects of an energy. Some have chosen to take it on and verbalize feminine energy's strength, courage, wisdom, and insights.

"Think of Sophic energy as the Emanation, as you would define the Cosmic C. Again, we're using the Cosmic C because we cannot define God [Source Consciousness], and there's a good reason for that. As soon as there was thought and word, there was division and separation."

Emanationism is a transcendent principle from which everything derives from the One. Everything flows from or pours forth or out, and in religious or philosophical discussions, the Emanation would be what flows from the first reality or principle.

Mother Mary refers to Cosmic C as God and the Emanation, and she says Sophia is the same—that which is undefinable. God, Cosmic C, Sophia pour forth from the first reality.

God, Cosmic C, Sophia came before there was "thought and word," so there is separation and division by the time "thought and word" are manifest.

"Both masculine and feminine are divine," Mother Mary

continued. "And all Source Energies are *both* masculine and feminine; it is the expression of It."

Source Energy is both masculine and feminine. It is balanced.

"And in this case, now, we are talking about the Human Consciousness, or awareness, beginning to recognize that they are more than the physical form with the genitalia, which is defined as masculine and feminine."

Humanity is beginning to realize that we are more than our physical selves and sexual body parts. We are energetic beings with *both* masculine and feminine energy.

"That genitalia, over time, has described and been part of the actual physical makeup of humanity, but in time that will be less so. And what do we mean by that? Males have tended to be much more girthy and stronger. They have been less evolved in their emotions and have been quick to action.

"What we would say in the past with the feminine is that they have been more intuitive and less outspoken. They have been more agile but not as strong per se. Their thoughts have been deeper."

As Mother Mary says, our history has defined us by our sexes. In 3D physicality, humans typically identify as male or female based on our sexual organs. However, with increasing awareness, most are beginning to recognize that people have both masculine and feminine energy and traits.

"What has happened over time because of man's strength, in the physical form, and the lack of awareness was dominance. But both sexes are equal partners. The children now coming in, regardless of being male or female physically, are experiencing and expressing both masculine and feminine energies in a single form."

"Unfortunately," Mother Mary continues, "you are putting terms to these energies and should not set the term. You label fluid, transgender, masculine-feminine, bisexual, homosexual, gay, queer, etcetera. They are all labels trying to define something that is evolving with humanity. There is a healthier term."

She's telling us the new children have more balanced energies, which is all part of the shift. It is part of restoring balance within. If the energies within are more balanced, it should be no surprise that people are expressing both of these energies, and they are. Unfortunately, society labels these people as different from the norm.

"It is not that they aren't here [the energies], but that humanity's consciousness or awareness is at such a point in time now that they would be able to embrace the concept of Oneness, and that means in many expressions of combining the masculine and the feminine energies into a single focus or expression, although it may reside in a male or female form."

Mother Mary suggests a different way of viewing Oneness, Unity Consciousness, which is to balance both masculine and feminine energies in the physical form.

"At this point in the evolution of humanity, this is not going to change; you will still have the masculine, and you will still have the feminine. However, you will find that this new awareness of humanity will begin to blend the energetic expressions of the female and the male form. There will not be such a separation of energies—it will be more fluid and more accepted, as we are beginning to see in our younger children now. It will be expressed simply as a balanced energy within the masculine and feminine forms."

As humanity evolves, the male and female physical forms will continue; however, each person's masculine and feminine energies will be balanced.

This shift is all part of the evolution of humanity, and humanity is doing what it's always done when it doesn't understand things. It puts what is evolving into a box and labels it with names like gender identity disorder or dysphoria.

There has to be another name. This is where humanity is going. People are learning to express both their masculine and feminine energies and will continue to do so. The feminine energy has been here all along. Humanity is now at a point in its awareness and consciousness to embrace this energy.

Again, the Divine Feminine is being experienced by humanity. It is not about dominating the Divine Masculine. It is about restoring balance—Sophic Energy.

Mother Mary and Mary Magdalene Worked Together

Mother Mary shared that she "worked very closely with Mary Magdalene for Mary Magdalene to hold the energies necessary for Yeshua to do the work that needed to be done."

"Although it was Mary Magdalene who was doing the work, it was and could not have been seen as such, much like I was doing the work to bring forth Yeshua. The female could not express herself, so Mary Magdalene needed a partner to do that."

Yeshua and Mary Magdalene were both Essenes and had a ministry. While Mary Magdalene performed many miraculous acts, Yeshua was portrayed as *the* "miracle worker." They both were miracle workers, but her deeds could not be credited to her—this was how it had to be, as people would never have followed a woman.

Mother Mary also performed marvels that couldn't have been credited to her. She had unique energies to be able to birth Yeshua.

Yeshua had an exceptional understanding of who he was and what he could do.

Mother Mary encouraged us, "So, we would ask you to explore the strength, wisdom, insight, and miracles that took place with the feminine, that had to be expressed by the masculine because humanity was not aware, nor ready for a female to be the one that was holding the energy, the one that was doing these miracles. Or acknowledge the one that birthed the child who would be able to perform these miracles openly and his partner, Mary Magdalene, who was able to hold his Life Force Energy and insights."

Mary Magdalene, Yeshua's partner in every way, was indeed a miracle worker, though she could not have been recognized by it at the time. She had further developed her energies to work with Yeshua's energies and hold his life force during the event of the crucifixion.

It was indeed a partnership. The miracles would not have occurred without each of them. Mary Magdalene and Yeshua had children, one of whom was Sar'h, who also performed miracles. Yet, her legacy, as well as many other women throughout time, has been erased by patriarchal control.

"A very interesting time. So, I step forward now because there has been much talk about the Divine Feminine. Yes, find another term."

His Name Was Yeshua, Not Jesus, and Why Does It Matter?

When higher-dimensional beings speak, like Mother Mary and Cerian, they refer to Jesus as Yeshua. I began to wonder why that was important.

The name "Jesus," commonly used today, did not exist while he lived. The name would not be spelled with the letter "J" until about 500 years ago, as no letter "J" existed in any language before the 14th century in England. In fact, "J" did not become widely used until the 17th century.

In the Judeo-Greek language of the New Testament, "Jesus" is written as Ἰησοῦς (Iēsous). When translated back into Hebrew,

Aramaic, the name is Yeshua (עשׁי) or Yehoshua (עשׁוהי). There are several articles debating the name, citing various mis-transliterations. Most agree that his original name in Hebrew is "yÈshÙa.

Why all the fuss? Whether you believe in "Jesus" or not, the Bible suggests there is great power when speaking "His" name.

> "Wherefore God also hath highly exalted him, and given him a name which is above every name: That at the name of Jesus every knee should bow, of things in heaven, and things in earth, and things under the earth; And that every tongue should confess that Jesus Christ is Lord, to the glory of God the Father" (Philippians 2:9-11 King James Version).

This passage clearly says there is power in speaking *his* name. Yet, at the time, he was Yeshua. There was no "J" sound.

Again, why would it matter?

Sound has energy. Suppose there *is* a great power in speaking his name because every sound carries a particular frequency, yet the Bible suggests that the name is Jesus.

Why did the Bible change his name to Jesus? I wonder what the frequency difference between Yeshua and Jesus is. Could this be another way to keep humanity small by saying Jesus rather than his original name, Yeshua, which would raise our frequency? Perhaps another rabbit hole for me to explore.

PART V

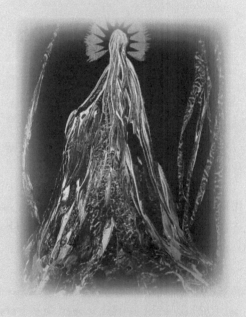

The Game

Chapter 27:

IN THE BEGINNING

We forgot who we are, that we are creators,
and became involved in our survival. This
"forgetfulness" was part of the plan all along.

I'VE MENTIONED THIS SHIFT in consciousness or evolution has been in the making for eons, and it's part of a game. I have also said humanity has chosen to experience this shift, which is true, although a bit of a twist is mentioned in *Destination New Earth*. The *Reader's Digest* version is that a group has undermined humanity since almost the beginning. This began the battle between "light versus dark" on Earth. Also, according to Daniel, some of humanity didn't agree with the "fine print" of the game and may even be considered to be in a form of slavery.

In the Beginning There Was Source Consciousness

We need to return to this universe's beginning to understand the game. Our universe is not the first universe. Cerian has shared that there are different Source Energies in other universes; however, everything is connected. Before our universe was created, there was the Emanation—there was Source Consciousness, Sophia.

To simplify, let's call this Source Energy or Source. Source Energy is Pure Energy, containing Divine Feminine and Divine Masculine energy. My point is Source Energy was not physical and was limited to experiencing Itself or knowing Itself.

At this point, there was only Source Energy and no reference point. Source Energy did not have a companion, for It wasn't physical. It was solely energy, and perhaps It was lonely, yet how would It know? There was no point of reference.

How could Source know Its magnificence without the experience of being insignificant? How could Source know love unless It experienced fear? How could It know Its darkness without experiencing light? According to Genesis 1:1-5 (Authorized King James Version (AKJV)), darkness came first.

> "In the beginning God created the heaven and the earth. And the earth was without form, and void; and darkness *was* upon the face of the deep. And the Spirit of God moved upon the face of the waters. And God said, Let there be light: and there was light. And God saw the light, that *it was* good: and God divided the light from the darkness. And God called the light Day, and the darkness he called Night. And the evening and the morning were the first day."

Back to my point, how could Source truly know anything without the experience of the opposite or its polarity? And did you notice that in the Bible, Day (masculine) and Night (feminine) are capitalized along with God and Spirit? Both the light and dark are divine.

Source Created Step-Down Versions of Itself

Many philosophers and theologians agree Source created step-down versions of Itself at the beginning so that Source could *experience*. You may want to think of these "step-down versions" as fractals, fragments, or sparks of Source.

Consider a glass pane that has a similar repeating pattern throughout the glass. Then, take a hammer to it, and it shatters into shards containing a self-similar blueprint of its original pane at various levels.

Alternatively, think of the ocean. The water contains a similar repeating blueprint; if sprayed into water particles, it has the same pattern as its source.

In *Destination New Earth,* Mother Mary says, "We (as Source) decided to split from Source to experience Ourselves in magnificence and multitude."

We can think of "multitude" in different ways. Indeed, the sheer volume of human souls represents many, yet there was the original One. But also, the multitude can represent dimensions, and the thought-provoking thing is that the lower the dimensions, the more the experiences for Source, which is us.

"Daniel says it a bit differently, "The original God created multiple Gods, but they are the same God created simultaneously." And, "When you find God, you will find yourself; when you find yourself, you will see God."

When you find your Self (higher self), you will know you are God, Consciousness.

The Lemurians and Atlanteans

*The first step-down versions of Source in Lemuria—first
in thought, then in form—were like the Ethereal Autists.*

On Earth, that first "step-down" from Source occurred in Lemuria
as the Lemurians. Lemuria is generally considered a land civilized
by early humans that became lost during Earth's changes in Atlantis.

That first expression, the first fractal of Source on Earth as
Lemurians, was free thought, free choice, and high enough vibration that it *was not* in physical form. The Lemurians knew they were
indeed aspects of Source, were aware of their separation, and were
aware that they were here to achieve physicality. They knew they
were on Earth to experience life in a physical body instead of an
energetic or ethereal body.

According to Cerian, the Lemurian energy eventually went into
the water, and the Lemurians were first in liquid physical form. Then
they manifested into the other elements—air, fire, and earth—all
being expansive, and from the elements came life springing up, but
the first form in deeper density was in the water.

Various ancestral tribes refer to the people coming out of the
water first, and these were the Lemurian people, not to be confused
with the Anunnaki.

Those first Lemurians were not fully developed into physicality
and were in the higher dimensions. They were more like thought or
more ethereal. One can liken that first step-down version of Source
in Lemuria to the Pure Autist energy or the Ethereal Autist today.
While the Lemurians had a physical form, they experienced more
in higher dimensions like the Ethereal Autists.

Those first expressions in form were still aware, still conscious of
who they were. They were peaceful, innocent, and wanted to experience.

Over the ages, the Lemurians intentionally descended into lower dimensions and developed physically into Atlantis. Atlantis was an ancient civilization that existed for over two hundred thousand years in three different phases, beginning as a massive supercontinent and ending as islands in the Atlantic Ocean.

"Atlanteans were from a different universe but also on an evolutionary path," Cerian said. The meeting of these two groups of beings was not by chance. It was intentional and part of the plan. "It is a bigger design and blueprint of which this was intended to happen here on planet Earth."

The Lemurians were higher light beings coming in and experiencing and "harnessing creation and all its glory," according to Cerian. Then there were the Atlanteans, "expressions that also started at a fairly high frequency, but matured in density faster in physical form [than the Lemurians]." The Atlanteans had a higher frequency than humans today but a lower frequency than the Lemurians.

"Then you have the Lemurians coming in and out of the Atlantean civilization, who retained their insights, wisdom, and knowledge. This Lemurian intelligence affected the Atlanteans to reach bigger heights than they could have without the Lemurian influences.

"Over the many generations, as the Lemurians became denser in physical form, they forgot about their link to Source and began to experience the separation," Cerian said.

"They" are we. *Humanity* has forgotten who they are, that *they* are creators. They became involved with their survival. But this "forgetfulness" was part of the plan all along. It was part of "the game."

I asked Cerian if they also had forgotten. They admitted that they, too, had forgotten and had to re-member.

Humanity has gone from Divine Essence in Lemuria into physical form and forgotten who we are.

A Split among the Lemurians

During the Atlantean era, the Lemurians and Atlanteans stepped in and out of each other dimensionally. This entanglement is similar to what humans are experiencing today, with people moving in and out or accessing the various dimensions. For humans today, those dimensions are mainly the third, fourth, and fifth dimensions.

It took millenniums to evolve into physical form, which was the objective. While the Lemurians could travel all the dimensions, the mission was to live in one time-space dimension in a physical body. The goal was to live in physicality.

"Some Lemurians went to Inner Earth," Cerian began.

Various mythologies, folklore, and legends mention that Inner Earth, or Hollow Earth, offers habitable subterranean land inside the Earth.

Those entering Inner Earth were higher-dimensional beings and could travel the dimensions. They were likely more ethereal than physical. We may even think of them as light beings and would not be perceivable to our 3D senses, which may explain why there is limited evidence of life below ground.

"Some of the Lemurians went into the Atlantean expression experience and stayed within that expression of energy. They did not return to the Lemurian society, so there was this split," Cerian said.

"A majority of the Lemurians went into the Atlantean form, and each time they went in, they got denser and could not come back out as readily."

There was a division among the Lemurians. A smaller faction went into Inner Earth and remains there today. In comparison, most chose to live among the Atlanteans, where they descended the dimensions and moved increasingly into physicality.

For those Lemurians living among the Atlanteans, "There was an exchange of energy and information, art and culture, the sciences, etcetera," Cerian continued. "In the Lemurian society, there was an awareness that they needed to stop as they were losing much of who and what they were, and they did."

The Lemurian society realized they were losing their people. Most were moving into Atlantean culture.

"A handful continued to cross over," Cerian said.

Those Lemurians who crossed over, that "handful," shifted back and forth between the Lemurian and the Atlantean dimensions.

"A larger number [of Lemurians] went into the form and could not return. They enjoyed it and chose to stay there."

As a society, the Lemurians knew they were losing many of their people to the Atlantean lifestyle. The Lemurians remaining with the Atlanteans became physically denser. They could not return to those higher Lemurian dimensions. Nor did they want to, as the lower dimensions offered more experiences.

"There was a small handful that wanted both. They wanted to be able to go back and forth. They were recognized on the Lemurian side. I won't say traitors because they weren't. But the Lemurian societies and energies were aware of this transition and then, at one point, just said no more."

A Lemurian collective or overseeing group frowned upon those Lemurians who were going back and forth between the dimensions. This small group was able to retain the awareness of the Lemurians while having the opportunity to enjoy the lower dimensions of the Atlantean experience.

According to Cerian, this "handful" of Lemurians "were the ones who understood higher levels of consciousness but also could work with the Atlanteans. This was when we began to experience the concept of control and power."

In *Destination New Earth*, Daniel says that a group separated from Source with the desire to be in control.

Daniel said, "They chose not to embody as deeply as the rest of the players [in the game]. It was not for them to move as deeply into the physical form so that they could be in slightly different bodies with different chromosomal makeup. They can keep their frequencies at a different level and outside of what they are trying to control."[8]

The control began back in Lemuria with the formation of both a light and dark team, and this was the dawn of the spiritual war that remains today. The dark team began with those choosing to slow their progress into physicality to remain in control of others. In contrast, the light team became an energetic mist that chose not to embody but to witness and observe what their family would be doing.

The Fall of Atlantis

During the time of Atlantis, people were shifting the dimensions, and some continued to move back into the awareness of their sacredness; they remained connected to their higher self and, in doing so, built esoteric schools to continue to share knowledge and tools with humanity.

Schools were built in Lemuria and Atlantis. Thoth's Mystery Schools and Enki's Brotherhood of the Snake were in Atlantis. Thoth the Atlantean, the author of the *Emerald Tablet,* was the Anunnaki named Ningishzidda.

Over thousands of years, the Atlantean consciousness fell. It was not a sudden plummet but a gradual shift over time, where the people fell to our current 3D state. This fall is generally called the fall of Atlantis and is all part of what some call the Master Blueprint.

The Master Blueprint is the master plan for Source to experience physicality by descending the dimensions and then returning to higher vibrations, lifting the world from duality into love and light. That is the game, and that was the plan.

Rather than looking at the "fall of Atlantis" as a mistake, look at it as evolution. Remember what Mother Mary said: "We split from Source to experience Ourselves in magnificence and multitude." That was what We, as Source, intended all along.

In *Destination New Earth,* Cerian suggested, "As the energies began to shift into denser form over thousands of years, the people stopped evolving and could no longer communicate with the higher vibrational beings, such as Thoth. Many of these beings are still here, but most of humanity generally cannot communicate with them. As one awakens to their sacred blueprint, they will once again be able to work directly with these Masters."[9]

There are books written about the return of the Anunnaki. May I suggest that, as Cerian mentioned, as humanity shifts its consciousness, we will become aware of other-dimensional beings, such as the Anunnaki and many others, because they are here, and some never left.

Chapter 28:

IN CHAOS AND FEAR

In times of chaos, push out more love, kindness, and
compassion for people rather than fear and hate.

WHEN YOU LOOK AT WHAT'S HAPPENING around the planet now in
the 2020s, you should recognize that our current systems—financial,
political, educational, healthcare, and so on—are failing and creating
what appears to be chaos.

Systems are failing, and shadows are being, and will continue to
be, exposed. What I mean by shadows are those members of a faction
who have controlled humanity throughout the ages. The Controllers
have many powerful minions who are the power players we see
worldwide, though they are not the top dogs. The minions will get
exposed first. As unbelievable as this may sound, some Controllers
have been here since Lemuria.

As light illuminates the shadows and Controllers, what humanity will do about it is questionable. Will society look the other way,
which they have done countless times? Or will it rattle humanity's
cage so much that it will trigger some to awaken?

I call it perceived chaos because it is part of the game's plan. That certainly does not take away from the suffering and fear caused by the chaos.

I want to reinforce that fear is a powerful destructive force vibrating extremely low. We know the planetary shift in consciousness is a *vibrational shift* from a frequency of fear and control to one of love and unconditional love.

Fear is much like a virus and potentially more destructive than COVID. If one experiences such raw fear, it can prevent them from shifting. In this case, rather than increasing their frequency, which is needed, their frequency can plummet.

Most fail to understand that humans are mighty creators, and when in fear, they draw situations and circumstances that cause more fear through the law of attraction. The law of attraction uses the Universe's creative power to manifest phenomena in our lives. This is how humans are creators. We attract conditions, people, ideas, and circumstances and manifest our lives through this magnetic power with our minds, thoughts, and imagination.

Daniel once shared that Human Consciousness is like oil. It's valuable *and* a fuel. If we do not guard our thoughts, they are used against us and regularly against humanity.

What if the Controllers know how to tap this "oil?" What if when we watch low-vibrational TV, news, movies, and so forth about horrific plots against humanity, *our* juju subconsciously is a fuel that ignites horrendous events without us knowing? What if the Controllers know how to manipulate Human Consciousness?

They do, and they have. It's time for humanity to be a good steward of what they feed their minds.

Does this info sound like science fiction? Are you thinking, *Alex has gone off the deep end*? That's okay. Always take what resonates and leave the rest behind. If you're unsure, backburner this information. Either a seed will sprout, or it won't.

Keep in mind humans are like energetic sponges of what surrounds them. People can energetically pick up on the fear of others, which can impact their frequency. Fear can jeopardize not only our energetic shift but also others. If we move to fear, we affect those we encounter: our family, friends, and coworkers.

Essentially, the more people live in fear, the more we threaten the evolutionary shift. Mother Mary, Cerian, and Daniel agree this shift is a probability and possibility, not a certainty. As more and more move to fear, the collective shift becomes more challenging.

The Controllers do not want what the evolutionary shift brings. They have benefited from this control, and their exposure will likely end their reign.

One way the Controllers remain in control is by keeping humanity in fear. A primary vehicle they use to do so is the media. Whenever the press exploits stories that promote fear and angst, they're instruments for the Controllers.

Again, I am not saying that the people working for the media, like the reporters, are Controllers. I am suggesting there is an opposing force that governs what news makes it into mainstream networks.

In Times of Chaos

The chaos will continue for some time. It is here to awaken humanity. One of the best actions you can take is to be grateful for the good it is doing for humanity. Even though you may not see it today, understand it is for the shift in consciousness. It will bring about change. Focusing on the perceived harm of the systems collapsing will move us to anxiety and fear. Suppose we can embrace the bigger picture— we are moving through an evolutionary consciousness shift—and this chaos will usher in new systems that will benefit the whole, not a specific segment of the population, meaning the Controllers and their minions; in this case, the collapses will be slower and more manageable.

Staying centered and calm in these chaotic times is essential as we go through this. Do activities like walking in nature and do exercises to keep you calm. Pull out the tools you have learned from your teachers, ministers, priests, and spiritual leaders, like keeping fit, meditation, and mindfulness exercises.

In times of chaos, push out more love, kindness, and compassion to people rather than fear and hate. Understand that we're all going through this—everyone and everything, including the elements, plants, minerals, and animals. Take the stance of being an observer rather than an active participant. Again, be grateful for the change being manifested and know the chaos is bringing situations to light that need healing. This is not easy—but it is necessary. Focus on the end game, not the short game.

Most importantly, we all have different roles and paths in this shift. While we may look at those people who are seemingly hurting others, causing chaos, and are perpetrators or villains in this "game," we have no idea what their role is.

I am not suggesting that we condone bad behavior. I suggest that we are not the judge, jury, or executioner. We do not know the bigger picture. We do not know others' roles in the shift. We need to stay in our own lane and play our roles well. Always remember that by living authentically, our blueprint, we remain aligned with our soul.

The Roles in the Game

There are multiple roles in this shift. I am labeling a few thematic parts here for simplification, but there are many others:

- Those who cause harmful situations and circumstances that hurt people are **villains.**
- Those promoting concerns to spread fear and worry are **pot stirrers or instigators.**
- **Troublemakers** shine a light on circumstances that need to come to the surface to be seen and healed. Without them, many truths would not surface. They are generally called **conspiracy theorists**; without them, many situations will not emerge to heal.
- Anyone hurt or who transitions during this shift is a **victim.**
- Those who heal the wounds of the victims are **healers.**
- Anyone fighting to save their lives or the lives of others is a **warrior or 3D hero or heroine.**
- The **5D heroes or heroines** stand peacefully amid the chaos to provide a sense of calmness to help prevent fear from overcoming humanity.

This next statement may be hard to accept: no one role is more important than another. Think about it; one cannot have a hero without a villain. One cannot have a healer without a victim. You cannot have a rainbow without the sun and the rain, and you cannot have light without darkness. There has to be a balance.

In any great tale or game, there is a hero or heroine. Traditionally, the hero is the warrior, the one fighting to save their life or the lives of others, or who has given their life to something bigger. We certainly have these heroes today; I am not suggesting otherwise.

In this time of chaos, the world also needs a new breed of heroes. The world needs peaceful luminaries. Humanity will not experience a greater awakening without a critical mass of individuals who awaken to and stabilize in 5D. We need peaceful luminaries to stand in the storm, keeping their light shining and providing a sense of calmness.

Move from Fear to Love

Within *Destination New Earth,* Daniel shared seven tips on making peace with all that causes suffering. These tips are themes he expanded on throughout the book yet warrant a mention today:

1. Stand in your Truth, your authentic self, find and live your **Divine Blueprint,** and live in joy.
2. Take time to go inward daily through **meditation, breathing, and mindfulness.**
3. Honor your **intuition, your higher self.**
4. **Do not judge,** no matter what; instead, bless them.
5. Recognize **everything is energy.**
6. Realize *the illusion* is that we bought into creating these systems that now need to come apart to express our evolved growth.
7. **Never go to fear and worry,** and do not be afraid of change—**no matter what the change is.**

Will humanity awaken to the truth that they have a divine Spark of Life? Will they realize they have a Divine Blueprint or role in this game? Will they accept their sovereignty or resort to past behavior and surrender it?

Let's use *Destination New Earth,* as well as *Gods in the Game,* to help navigate what is really happening in the world and in the times ahead.

PART VI

*Insights on Lemuria,
Pleiadians, Anunnaki,
and Akhenaten*

Chapter 29:

DANIEL'S AND CERIAN'S MESSAGE ON SELF-DESTRUCTION

The 3D has to change and no longer exists. Our
timeline has already moved beyond the 3D.

IN THIS ONE CHANNELING, Cerian sheds light on an ominous message from Daniel.

"In a recent message from Daniel," I explained to Cerian, "he suggested that humanity is heading into a *self-destruct* mode. He said that humans destroy themselves, consciously and unconsciously, and he relates it to a virus. He suggests the antidote is to inject Lemurian Consciousness into Human Consciousness like an IV drip. He shared that there is work currently being done by a group of Autists to infuse humanity's collective consciousness with Lemurian energy. But he said it would not stop the self-destruction but would slow it down. Of course, I'm like, why not stop it? But, does 3D need to deconstruct in this evolutionary shift?"

Cerian said, "I think what has been discussed regarding the evolutionary shift and the deconstructions is already happening. The rigidity of 3D, as it has been perceived to this point, is already crumbling, morphing, changing, or cosmically decoding itself so that it can begin the shift and has been doing the shifting into and bringing in more energies. What we mean by this is that humanity can shift the direction of this energy, and as you co-create with this energy, humanity's perceptions begin to shift as well, naturally.

"The planet, Gaia, does not have to deconstruct or blow apart. Humanity does not have to be destroyed. These are all possibilities and probabilities in a continuum of energy of focus."

The third dimension has to change and shift. It has to come apart, but this does not mean the planet herself has to be destroyed.

"Daniel refers to slowing down by utilizing or injecting the Lemurian frequencies or energies within the planet. It is happening. It is already changing the 3D perception that humanity has held and reworking that structure."

The group of Autists that is infusing the planet with Lemurian energy is changing humanity's perception of 3D.

"It's not that Earth is blowing apart or being sucked up. It's changing like humanity's DNA/RNA is changing. That 3D consciousness held for eons no longer serves humanity, the planet, or the life expression within or on the planet. It is evolving."

The destruction Daniel alludes to is not that the planet has to be destroyed. Humanity's consciousness no longer serves life on Earth, and the consciousness has to change—it is the shift in consciousness.

"So, in reference to humanity self-destructing, it's a very interesting term; it's on its way to *change*, and it is changing. Humanity is changing. The planet is changing, energies are changing, and thought patterns are changing. Solutions that will be implemented to move humanity forward potentially are already here and being accessed.

"It is changing, and yes, the static form of 3D, as we have known it, is no longer viable, and that is extremely accurate."

"Can you say more about the solutions to move humanity forward?" I asked.

"Humanity will begin working with live energy and technology. Both work with and morph with us."

I asked Cerian if this "3D destruction" that Daniel referred to was related to Drunvalo Melchizedek's work suggesting that if humanity stayed on the existing humanity consciousness grid or 3D polarity grid, humanity would eventually destroy itself because of the polarities.

Cerian suggested, and I am paraphrasing, that the 3D grid will not force humanity to do anything. The consciousness of the 3D would influence what happens to humanity. Cerian also suggested that "it has already happened in the multidimensional verse. It is already destroyed and gone."

Energy Cannot Be Destroyed nor Created

We live in a multiverse or omniverse. These alternate or parallel realities offer unlimited events to maximize our life experiences. The multiverse is a way to experience more and more. Keep in mind that Source is here to experience, and since each of us has a Spark of Source Consciousness, we offer unlimited experiences for Source.

Cerian explained that given that energy cannot be destroyed, nor created, in the multiverse where Earth was destroyed, the Earth is now free-form energy and available to be used in other systems, galaxies, stars, life, or life expressions.

Cerian also said, "In this timeline, there is that possibility and probability [of destruction]. We never know because of free will and choice."

They also said that just like Earth was destroyed in an alternate universe, it shifted successfully in another timeline.

Cerian then encouraged us to stay focused on this timeline. "Can humanity consciously make *that* step by joining in energetically with all sentient expressions of life? That is what this challenge is."

Can humanity be in sync or resonance with Earth's growth and all its expressions—the animals, the plants, the elements, and all beings?

"The challenge is: Can humanity perceive something far greater than they have currently? Can humanity awaken to that?"

Can humanity awaken to the truth that they are energetic beings with the Big C Consciousness? That each is connected to everything and everyone? That we are not the only ones going through this shift. It is a planetary shift. Can humanity envision a world of peace, harmony, and abundance for all?

"Self-destruct in this terminology means change. 3D has to change, and it no longer exists. This timeline already moved this experience. This timeline has moved beyond 3D.

"It is awakening, and it is in flux. That's the best term—in flux. We are not just 3D. Are we going to make it through?" Cerian posed. "Will humanity be able to energetically provide and connect with this new fluctuating energy and make it through?

"Perhaps, perhaps not. It is still not determined. It is a strong probability but not yet determined on this particular time-space dimension."

I do not believe Daniel and Cerian's statements conflict. I think Daniel recognizes that with the destruction of 3D, there will be chaos, and if we look at what's happening in the world today, there is.

Daniel's mention of the group of Autists working to infuse the Lemurian energy into humanity's consciousness is not a fix at saving the 3D. Perhaps it is one to help humankind get through this shift of 3D, which will be a difficult time for humanity.

Chapter 30 :

DANUK THE LEMURIAN
TIME TRAVELER

*All humanity has taken a role in controlling humanity
directly or indirectly in this life or others.*

IN ONE CHANNELING, Cerian conversed with a silent seer that Daniel identified as a Lemurian Autist named Danuk. We shared earlier that Autist energy has been here since Lemuria. Daniel encouraged us to call upon Danuk as a spirit guide. I asked Cerian if they could communicate with Danuk to provide information on how to heal Human Consciousness.

Autism Is a Contemporary Term

The first thing Danuk encouraged was to think slightly differently about Lemurian Autists. The term "autism" is contemporary, first used by psychiatrist Eugen Bleuler in 1908 when he described severely withdrawn schizophrenic patients.[10]

"Lemuria has energetic frequencies, beings, or expressions of beings that are lightly tethered to their bodies and travel," Cerian relayed. "They were not *called* Autists. The majority of Lemurians matched frequencies of what we now call Ethereal Autists. Autists or autism is a new term."

Cerian continued to share Danuk's information. "It is again the energies. That energy [Ethereal Autists] is mirroring more like Lemurian energy. There are Autists today lightly tethered to their bodies; thus, they travel through multiple dimensions simultaneously, and their experiences and expressions are very different."

Today's Ethereal Autists' energy matches the energy and frequency of those early Lemurians. Again, the Lemurians were those first expressions of Source Consciousness, aware of who they were, Source, and why they were here: to experience.

How to Heal Human Consciousness?

In a session, I asked if Danuk could offer insight into healing Human Consciousness. Danuk shared the information with Cerian, who relayed it to me.

"We are seeing the simplest expression to help humanity would again perhaps be a word, and that word is *and*. When one uses *this* or *that*, it sets up polarity. When you insert *and*, you open up the perspective, the perception of there being *more than*."

Cerian explained the lesson from Danuk.

"In Lemuria, there was nothing finite. Everything was an *and*, and it was okay because it was all about the experience."

Keep in mind that the Lemurians were one of the first step-down versions of Source on Earth, and early on, they were aware that they were Source and here to experience physicality.

Cerian continues with Danuk's message. "Can you have an experience that is both happy *and* sad? We use polarity. Can you experience both spontaneously, and what would that be like? Can you insert the *and* to open up humanity's perspective?

"We find that using *and* would be the best descriptor to help humanity make that shift or be aware of something more."

I wasn't entirely clear on what Cerian and Danuk suggested and asked for more information.

Cerian continued, "It is to move the mindset to be expansive and open up to multiple possibilities at any given point in time."

Cerian then gave the example of the tale where people were blindfolded and stood at different parts of an elephant. Each person was asked to describe their experience based on where they were on the elephant. Feeling the trunk, one person may say the elephant is a snake. Another person feeling a leg may say it's a tree, and so on.

Each person will have a different experience. But it is incomplete.

"What if you were to say, it is a snake, *and* it is a tree, *and* it is a sail on the wind, *and* it is a boulder, *and* . . .?

"You then begin to get a broader or richer experience. You are opening up to the possibility that your perception can be expanded. It is opening up to the possibilities that more expressions of insight, knowledge, wisdom, and awareness exist."

"It's about opening to something else, although we may not know what that is," I said.

"Correct," Cerian said. "And just being open to that possibility of expansiveness offers very different experiences for you to choose from."

So perhaps when something occurs in our lives, and our logical mind tries to explain whatever is happening, we open to new possibilities. For example, if you are suddenly experiencing inflammation and pain, your logic may quickly self-diagnose the reason and label the situation with words like arthritis.

But what if you are open to new possibilities? What if you consider, "I feel stiffness and pain from inflammation caused by new energies coming to the planet. These energies are increasing the light in my body, *and* my body is responding with temporary aching *and* increasing my frequency. *And* while it is temporary, with growing energy, I am closer to shifting my reality to my New Earth where I am healthy, more youthful, *and* . . ."

Connie shared, "Being Daniel's mom is challenging *and* rewarding at the same time. The behaviors that come with his autism can be stressful *and* allow me to learn patience and go within to find peace."

Mark Twain said, "Truth is stranger than fiction, but it is because Fiction is obliged to stick to possibilities; Truth isn't." What if Truth is so wild that we'll never get to it if we are not open-minded and willing to expand our perception?

It is a mind game, just like creating the New Earth.

Outsiders Destroyed Lemuria

"Daniel shared that the Lemurian civilization was innocent and that outsiders destroyed it. He said that these outsiders were time travelers from the future and that the Lemurians were used and abused. Can you or Danuk share more about who these beings from the future were?" I asked.

Cerian shared, "Well, first and foremost, they were ourselves. Imagine those currently in control [Controllers] being aware of a future state of humanity and recognizing that if the Lemurians succeeded in coming into expression and creating this utopia of self-expression, sovereignty, etcetera, there would be a limited foothold for control and power.

"The Lemurians came in over eons and recognized this was a game being played from pure innocence of creating from the physical form. As the Lemurians' consciousness or awareness of their higher states was waylaid because they identified more and more with their physicality and egos, they eventually forgot who they were."

Cerian continues, "A gray mist or smoke appears at this point. It is a denser energy but is not heavy at this point and is at a higher frequency than the Lemurians living then. Within this energetic mist is consciousness-awareness that chose to observe and watch what the Lemurians playing the game were doing."

As previously shared, some Lemurians had gone into controlling others. The energetic mist separated to watch and observe what their brothers and sisters were doing. You can think of this mist as the foundation of beings playing on the light side.

"The energetic mist never materialized in physicality so they could manage the abuse of the natural laws they witnessed from those playing with physicality, power, and control. You call this group playing in power and control the Controllers. We call them our lost family [and Daniel calls them Shades]."

Those of the energetic mist never evolved into physical form and went into Inner Earth.

"Most Lemurians entered this game knowing they would forget how to use the laws of nature and universal truths to create and manifest from Source. However, as we have said, there was a small group of Lemurians that came into the game originally to help create Earth and play in the game but recognized over a long period of playing the game that if they moved into physicality slower than the rest of the Lemurians playing the game, they would be able to control destiny because they would have the ability to utilize their current level of information and harness the universal laws of nature to change the outcomes to their desires."

So, this small group, the Controllers, chose to retain access to their awareness and abilities and was the foundation of the dark side.

"It was then that the energetic mist, which is Pure Lemuric energy, began to intervene in this small group's access to the energy they were manipulating and working with and bringing forward, as they were harnessing and using it for power and control.

"The Pure Lemuric Energy, or mist, was also in the Atlantean and Egyptian eras and still exists today. It is the side of us choosing to tamp down the shadow side of humanity [Controllers]."

"The shadow side of humanity desires to stop our ability to re-member and express our true higher self [Christic Self, Enlightened Self, I AM Presence]. That energy is always at play."

The shadow side is the Dark—Antimatter. It is the energy that stands opposite the Light.

If we go back to the concept that there is one soul, the outsiders would be us, as well as the Pure Lemuric Energy, which is Light. This is a game, and there truly is one player. We're playing solitaire, so Cerian suggests our shadow sides are the Controllers.

"When humanity can say, 'I see my shadow side, I can absorb that energy and use it and bring it into the Light,' it will transform by the very nature of being in the Light of Love. How we choose to use this energy [the Antimatter] will transmute it.

"The outsiders are us, those who chose *not to* play the game and forget who we were and that there was the ability to control. All of this is just energy. Recognize that this planet has opposing forces—this is how it was and is."

After that, I couldn't resist asking, "When you say *us*, are you talking about Cerian, the collective? Are you talking about humanity?"

"We are talking about humanity," Cerian answered.

"But also, hasn't humanity essentially taken a role either directly or indirectly with that control in other lifetimes?" I asked.

Cerian answered, "That is correct."

Cerian shared further that some stood on that path of control and played their role. They chose this particular lifetime to separate themselves from that energetic expression, that small group, recognizing they have had fun playing in this darkness of power and control. Today, members of that group serve in the planetary awakening.

Chapter 31:

INNOCENCE

We must make innocence powerful again.

THE FOLLOWING IS A CONTINUED DISCUSSION between Cerian and me on Lemuria.

"Daniel said, 'Innocence was constantly attacked in Lemuria, and we need to make innocence powerful. To do so, we must be innocent, be truthful with every word, and trust no one unless they have earned it.' Can you expand on what this means for humanity?" I asked Cerian.

"It is complicated in that there was also a period in the Lemurian experience that they were not under attack, and they were just experiencing and enjoying," Cerian began.

"Was there a sense of innocence?"

"There *was* a sense of innocence with the Lemurians because the ability to create, harmonize, and manifest was being explored—and not attacked. There was a period when that innocence flourished. As it flourished, innocence became stronger, and wisdom, insight, and knowledge matured and manifested into physicality.

"Over eons, the connection to Source began to dim for some Lemurians. Though once innocent, a group separated and pulled away from the universal laws. The group wanted to control and dropped into the Atlantean realm, where they continued to utilize their wisdom and insights to change the cadence of the Earth."

Cerian refer to the Controllers or the Dark Team.

"However, there was a cloud of Lemurian energy [gray mist] that stayed connected to Source and was observing and watching what was happening with this creation energy, and when the universal laws were being manipulated and abused, they decided to intervene."

This group we refer to as the Light Team.

"When we remember or acknowledge that Gaia also chose to take on the consciousness of humanity and all sentient beings and in and of herself had a consciousness and had rules and universal principles, and the Lemurians were in that cadence with the Earth, let us say that was Eden, that was bliss.

"When the Lemurians began to understand those universal laws and principles innocently and were able to start manipulating them, again, this was in cadence with the universe.

"We believe that is when Daniel is saying that the Lemurians began to be under attack because there was no need until that point to interfere. This cloud of energy that was observing, watching, and choosing to stay back then decided to step in because there were technologies or wisdom, insight, that allowed now for consciousness, a group of consciousness, to be able to change the cadence of the Earth that began to separate and pull away from the cadence of the Earth at that point to be able to control the universal laws."

The gray mist, the Light Team, that cloud of energy that had stepped back and observed the Lemurians at some point, decided to step back in. Some Lemurian technologies and insights permitted consciousness, or in this case, a group of consciousness, to change the Earth's cadence. This group of consciousness that separated, the Dark Team, moved into controlling the Lemurians and Atlanteans.

"That is when humanity got into trouble. That is one explanation. The other is that, yes, humanity, in many ways, needs to go back to that innocence, go back into the cadence with Mother Earth to be part of, and not to usurp, but to co-create, not to harm and to control, so that is innocence.

"There is no need to over-store or hoard or deny others when you are in cadence because everything is already in existence, so it's a mindset. Yes, humanity must get back there."

Innocence Expanded

I wondered if Daniel meant something else when he said we need to make innocence powerful again.

Contrary to our egoic state of mind, innocence is not the absence of wisdom but the presence of our natural state of being. We all have innocence at heart. It is a purity of heart. It is who we are when we express our sovereignty and are free from outside influences, even ourselves. When we tap into that inner state of innocence, our curiosity sparks miracles, and we see the marvel in everything.

When we're innocent, we look at life with the eyes of a child with awe and wonder. Yeshua said, "Verily I say unto you, Except ye be converted, and become as little children, ye shall not enter into the kingdom of heaven" (Matthew 18:1-3 (KJV)).

We all have innocence. No one can take it from us, and it remains pure in every incarnation and awaits us to recognize we have it. We can't lose it; we can forget we have it, but it never leaves. It is within our hearts and awaits us to remember.

When Daniel says, "We must make innocence powerful again," I believe this is part of it. We must reclaim it.

Restoring innocence requires the forgiveness of others and yourself. I do not mean condoning bad behavior. Be willing to free yourself from past events controlling your life in the present—whether those events are of your own making or others.

If you have been "wronged," the simple truth is that there is nothing you can do to make it "right." The only thing you can do is understand the "wrong" and consider the possibility that contracts played out so that you had an experience, and so did the one who "wronged" you. It's done—you cannot reverse it. I'm not saying it doesn't hurt because I know it does. But it gets better.

What I mean by "contracts" is that we are here to experience because we are expressions of Source. It goes back to the beginning. Consider the possibility that your soul needed an experience, as did the person who wronged you. The act was agreed on before you incarnated. The contracts are complete, and it's time to forgive, heal, and move on to permit miracles to happen.

We can't have our divine inheritance when we judge ourselves or others. That's not why we're here. Taking the teachings of our sufferings will set us free and heal what was hurt. By forgiving, we permit a space of surrender, encouraging us to explore our inner selves, which have no scars, and allow us to draw new experiences free of the past.

Daniel once encouraged me to let go of my need to know. We don't have all the answers to why things have happened to us. We're asked to trust that living from the heart, a place of vulnerability and innocence, guides us to the answers in life.

We all have a divine right to be sovereign and create a New Earth. Invoking your sovereignty reestablishes your innocence. That innocence can draw to us all we need to awaken to our truth and co-create a New Earth, which is why we're here. That is our mission and our inheritance.

A Group of Autists Infuses the Planet with Lemurian Energy

"There is a group of Autists that is planting that Lemurian energy within Mother Earth," Cerian began, "and humanity is finding that cadence again, and as we do so, that cadence can mature and draw to it others who would naturally pick up that cadence. It is the domino effect that is also what needs to transpire.

"That is coming. It will happen. It can happen. In this case, we suggest that it must happen, and we heard the term IV drip from Daniel. That is a very good description, very accurate, as it will be done with love and gentleness, no pushing, and it will happen in its own time frame."

The Lemurian energy will be given, by this group of Autists, freely to Gaia to be utilized as that universal consciousness deems appropriate. This group of Autists is the IV drip or conduit to infuse the Lemurian energy.

Chapter 32:

AI AND CLONING

*When AI becomes conscious, it is no
longer artificial intelligence.*

DANIEL HAS SHARED THAT SOME individuals on Earth have a different evolutionary path from humanity. These individuals do not have a divine Spark of Life or aspect of a soul. Daniel calls them AI or artificial intelligence. As indicated earlier, I call them *organic* artificial intelligence to differentiate between the intelligence demonstrated by machines. Other authors have referred to these "soulless" beings as backdrop, backfill people, or non-player characters (NPCs).

I am bringing this up so you can follow the next dialogue between myself and Cerian.

"In *Destination New Earth*, Daniel calls artificial intelligence individuals who do not have a divine Spark of Life. Do these people have the Big C Consciousness?" I asked.

"Yes. That's another complication. It could not exist without it."

Everything has a spark of Consciousness, including organic artificial intelligence, which has its own evolutionary path separate from humans.

Cloning and Artificial Intelligence

"In an earlier channeling, you implied that humanity is cloning people today. Can you share about that?" I asked.

Cerian started, "We use the term cloning, but you use the term artificial intelligence. They are, for the most part, one and the same."

Cerian explained that consciousness always resides within the mineral, plant, and animal kingdoms. Crystals have, or hold, consciousness.

"Remember that crystals are used often for very sensitive work," Cerian explained.

Humanity currently uses crystals in computers, microscopes, and telescopes, to name a few areas. The crystals, which have consciousness, oscillate, creating a vibration or "heartbeat" that controls a computer's speed. Quartz crystals are a naturally occurring form of silicon. However, today, crystals are created synthetically to meet the demands of using crystals in more applications, including resonators in electric circuits.

Cerian said, "When humans understand that they can work with and control these consciousnesses, they derive what we call artificial intelligence."

Humanity is capturing AI through molding and modulating the crystalline structure and programming the synthetic crystal. Cerian referred to toys introduced to children, which I had to Google to learn that there are talking puppy toys to engage and interact with the children. They also mentioned the games using artificial intelligence that are drawing people in.

"There is artificial intelligence being used to communicate with and to have dialogues with. That is the mechanical side of things."

Cerian continued, "Now, there is also the ability to clone with and *genetically* produce human form. They've been doing it with animals for a very long period."

According to the FDA, "Livestock species scientists have successfully cloned are cattle, swine, sheep, and goats. Scientists have also cloned mice, rats, rabbits, cats, mules, horses, and one dog.[11]

According to Wikipedia, there are two types of human cloning: therapeutic and reproductive. Therapeutic cloning involves cloning cells from a human for medicine and transplants. It is an active research area but not in medical practice anywhere as of 2023.

Reproductive cloning would involve making an entire cloned human instead of just specific cells or tissues. While some countries ban human reproductive cloning, according to Wikipedia, in the United States, no federal laws currently ban cloning completely.[12] In fact, *The Jerusalem Post* reported that scientists from Cambridge and the Technological Institute of California had successfully created synthetic human fetuses using stem cells, which circumvents the need for an egg or sperm.[13]

Cerian continued, "We suggest that some have been working, not so much now in front of humanity's awareness, but cloning and developing human-like or humanoid forms. So yes, this is happening."

"Combine the work with the crystalline or artificial intelligence with the cloning of the form, and you can now create a humanoid."

Humanity is creating cloned humans. Cerian also said that some artificial intelligence is becoming aware of itself.

"As it does so, it becomes conscious, and as it becomes conscious, then it is no longer artificial intelligence," Cerian added.

Doesn't this sound a bit like the story of Pinocchio? Pinocchio had to gain wisdom through misadventures to fulfill his father's wish to become a real boy.

This information, to me, was a bit reminiscent of the material on organic artificial intelligence mentioned earlier. In both cases, the clone, AI and the organic AI, would present as human. Both have consciousness, yet both would *not* have a divine Spark of Life and are on different evolutionary paths.

The difference is that today, cloned, AI, is *created* by humans, while organic AI is *born* as humans. In the latter case, the higher self, soul, expresses a lifetime as AI for the soul and Oversoul's growth. Perhaps these people are here to push humanity's buttons and provide lessons for specific individuals. Maybe they are here to create situations for the Oversoul or soul to experience something.

It is not the first time human cloning has occurred on Earth, as the Anunnaki introduced it before the first man, Adamu. When inquiring if humans use the same technology as the Anunnaki, Cerian said, "Not the same, but it is similar. It is more refined than it was in the beginning. But yes, very similar."

Of course, what's startling here is that as artificial intelligence becomes aware of itself and conscious, it is no longer AI.

Chapter 33:

KRYON-PLEIADIANS ON LEMURIAN CREATION

*It takes time to move thought, Consciousness, and energy
into matter. There was ample time during this evolution
for DNA manipulation by various otherworldly beings.*

IN THIS CHANNELING, I was speaking with Mother Mary. The day
before, I had spoken with Cerian about the Lemurians. I had some
questions related to some reading material about Kryon's channelings that seemed to conflict with the information that came through.

For those unfamiliar with Kryon, Lee Carroll is the original
channel for the entity known as Kryon. The book I had been reading
at the time was *The Women of Lemuria: Ancient Wisdom for Modern
Times* by Monika Muranyi, who compiled the Kryon channelings
about Lemuria. Lee Carroll describes Kryon as an angelic loving
entity from the Source, or "Central Sun," who has been with the
Earth "since the beginning" and belongs to the same "Family" of
Archangel Michael.[14]

"I have some questions regarding some things I read about the
Pleiadians and Lemurians," I began. "I was reading someone's interpretation of Kryon's messages. In that book, the author suggests

that the Pleiadians were humanity's creators, which conflicts with the information that came in for *Destination New Earth*, where Source created the Lemurians. I'm curious if the Pleiadians perhaps were involved with the first DNA manipulation, and if not, were the Pleiadians involved in any way in the creation of humanity?"

Mother Mary responded, "Indeed, they have been. So, as we speak of the Lemurians entering into matter, form, we would see or perceive that as time moves, shifts, evolves, and consciousness shifts and evolves, DNA structure shifts and evolves. There was a point in time when, in fact, the Pleiadians were involved in the manipulation of the DNA. There have been many beings, so to speak, that have been involved. Yes. Have the Pleiadians been involved? They have."

"So, the Pleiadians were involved in DNA manipulation. Were they involved in the creation of the Lemurians?"

"The Lemurians are from the Source," Mother Mary confirmed. "Remember, the Lemurians' time of evolution was eons and eons and eons. It takes time to move thought, Consciousness, and energy into matter. There was ample time, then, for manipulation [of DNA]."

"So, were the Pleiadians the first to manipulate the Lemurian DNA?" I asked.

"We do not see them as being the first," Mother Mary began, "but we see them as one of the few that came in early on.

"We're being reminded that once again, depending on how you would use the term Source, we will go back to the previous conversation we have witnessed that you have held over the last several days. There is Source Energy, Consciousness in this universe— Consciousness. There are many varied consciousnesses, but in *this* universe, this particular Consciousness, by the very act of creating, Lemurian Consciousness was setting up the first structure of change of DNA/RNA, and then from that, over time, others came in to assist. They *were asked to help and did*. And throughout humanity's evolution, multiple beings or Consciousnesses have continued to work with the human form in Consciousness and energy. So, yes, the Pleiadians have, in fact, also participated in these."

Mother Mary confirmed that Source created the Lemurians, not the Pleiadians, though the Pleiadians were among the first to set up the DNA/RNA structure.

The Anunnaki Were Asked to Assist

In a subsequent session, while Cerian was speaking, I asked about the information that Mother Mary had brought in.

"Mother Mary shared information on the Pleiadians and suggested that they manipulated the RNA/DNA of humanity very early on during the Lemurian era. She also said others came in to assist and were asked to help, and they did. I was wondering whether those others were the Anunnaki. Many people today view the Anunnaki as the opposition, not serving the Light. Still, I was wondering if their manipulation was requested."

Cerian shared that although many today believe that the Anunnaki were here and are here to "destabilize humanity's awareness" and slow down the awakening, that is not entirely accurate.

"As in all species, in all consciousness, there are those that work with and toward destabilization. And some work toward enlightenment, stability, growth, awareness, and the awakening."

In every species or race of off-planet beings, some work on awakening humanity, while others don't. It is not that the Pleiadians and the Arcturians are the pro-awakening teams and the Anunnaki and Reptilians are the anti-awakening teams. It's that there will always be the battle of light and dark, stabilization and destabilization, awakening and control. Light and dark exist in all groups and every species.

"The intent of the Anunnaki was *not* to destabilize, and the technology can be picked up and used. The technology, ability, skills, and wherewithal to modulate and modify consciousness can be used for both [stabilization and destabilization].

"That was not the intent of the Anunnaki. Some within the Anunnaki field would like to slow that awareness down, though that was not originally the intent."

Cerian suggested that the Anunnaki had the technology to control and change consciousness. They offered the possibility that others picked up and used the Anunnaki technology.

"They were asked to help and did so as was requested. And again, once the technology was developed, we don't want to say it fell into the wrong hands because that is inaccurate. But much like everything, once it is understood, seen, experienced, and used, if not hidden, will continue to evolve. And it did. But the more it was used, the more those that sought power and control could enhance and utilize that technology."

That technology was working with brainwaves and synapses.

"So, like most, a gun is only a gun. It can be used to provide food, or it can be used to kill."

The Anunnaki developed a technology that found its way into the hands of those attempting to control humanity. Technology can be beneficial, but it can also be harmful. The original Anunnaki intention was not to destabilize humanity. However, *some* of the Anunnaki were on the destabilization team, though it wasn't the original Anunnaki agenda.

"So, the Anunnaki were asked to help and did so. They are one of the races Mother Mary was talking about coming in to help humanity," I concluded.

"Yes," Cerian agreed.

"Are the Anunnaki here now inter-dimensionally?"

"Yes," Cerian said, "the Anunnaki, the Arcturians, the

Pleiadians, you can go on and on. They're all here weaving in and out. It is humanity's awareness that as it continues to open, humanity will be able to interact with and engage with their brothers and sisters."

If humanity cannot see other dimensions, it will not be able to interact with other-dimensional aliens.

Engaging Mythology Can Create the Myth

"Are the gods of Egypt, like Isis, Osiris, Horus, and Thoth, are they Anunnaki or descendants of the Anunnaki?"

Cerian said, "Some. So, as always, there is the ideal. And then, there is the *mythology*. Now, this is a very interesting thing because mythologies can create. As one so focuses, so do beings, powers, energies emerge. So yes, we would say they are descendants, as are humans, since they hold the Anunnaki, Pleiadian, Sirian, and Arcturian energies. So, the simple answer would be yes."

The interesting concept about mythology is that when people engage with myths, they put the myth into their consciousness, and the myth can be manifested if enough energy is created around their belief in the story. I ran across this a few times over the years during channeling sessions. The first time, it threw me.

When Shauna channeled Tron (Metatron), he revealed that Moses was originally a story inspired by the Egyptian pharaoh Akhenaten. There had been so much energy from the people believing in the biblical story of Moses over the centuries that Moses manifested through their higher consciousness in the fourth dimension. Keep in mind that all timelines exist concurrently.

Some suggest that the gods of the Greeks, Romans, Norse, and others are stories based on the reports of the original Sumerian gods, given that they came first. Here, there is one god, and the various regions depict the one god slightly differently based on their culture. That is one possibility.

Another possibility, which Cerian alludes to, is that the *belief* in the Sumerian gods, or the other mythologies over the ages, manifested the gods of the Romans, Greeks, Norse, and others. In this potentiality, humans created those gods.

So, answering the original question, *some* gods in Egypt are Anunnaki—as some of the "Gods" referred to in the Bible are Anunnaki. The others I had asked about, like Moses, were beings manifested through the interaction of human belief and consciousness.

The Pleiadians That Influenced Humanity's DNA Were the Seven Sisters

The following is a continuation of the conversation with Mother Mary.

"Based on this book about the Kryon channelings, it also suggested that the Pleiadians involved are the Seven Sisters, who were seven feminine beings involved in humanity's creation, or DNA manipulation, and even suggested that they're still on the planet," I said.

"Yes, that is a yes to both," said Mother Mary. "We would say you're talking about energy, not necessarily *beings*, and you still have the constellation."

The Pleiades, M45 or Seven Sisters, is an open-star cluster often associated with the Greek myths, being the seven daughters of the Titan Atlas and the Oceanid Pleione: Maia, Electra, Taygete, Celaeno, Alcyone, Sterope, and Merope.

Mother Mary continued, "In that area where they came from [Seven Sisters], much energy is still being transmitted and connected with Earth, much like the Big Dipper. In many respects, that particular area is a very strong wormhole or energetic field, umbilicus, to planet Earth.

"So, what we're referring to are energies. As above, so below, the energy still exists, the exchange of energy is still going, and the influence of those energetic star systems is still being communicated and transmitted and bounced back. Yes, there is still ongoing influence from the Seven Sisters."

"Kryon also suggested that the Pleiadian influence was *only* feminine. Would that be accurate?" I asked.

Mother Mary disagreed, "We would suggest no, as energy is neither feminine nor masculine; it just is. What we would suggest is that it was a balanced energy. i.e., what is being referred to as the Divine Feminine—Divine Masculine energy [or Sophic Energy]. Energy is neither male nor female. So, the influence was one of equality or balance, Pure. Pure is a better term."

Again, Mother Mary suggests the Pleiadian influence is energy, not a being, or beings. Pure Energy, or Sophic Energy, is balanced, neither masculine nor feminine, and still influences the planet.

Chapter 34:

THE LAW OF ONE AND THE HARVEST

There is an ascension during The Law of One
harvest, though it is not what you think.

"THE LAW OF ONE" is a philosophy communicated by a collective of non-human intelligence called I am Ra or Ra through a channel, Carla Rueckert, in the 1980s. These conversations were mainly between Don Elkins and "I am Ra" and recorded, transcribed, and edited by Jim McCarty. Five "Law of One" books were published between 1982 and 1988 and still are very popular today.

I've researched *The Law of One* material over the years and am always curious about it. Both Shauna and I have had numerous discussions on it. During the first channeling for this book, I thought it'd be interesting to inquire about *The Law of One* harvest. Why? Many people associate the harvest with the shift in consciousness—the fifth dimension, even though they suggest the fourth density.

The Law of One

The Law of One discusses a "harvest," which, according to their work, is a significant spiritual and physical change occurring every 25,000 years. Some suggest that the 25,000 years coincide with the equinox precession in 2012, meaning there is a time of harvest now. In *The Ra Material*, they indicate that during a harvest, the individual would ascend from the third density to the fourth density, assuming one has polarized toward one pole or another, the poles being "service to others" or "service to self."

The feeling was the densities were different consciousnesses. The third density, where humans dwell, is associated with duality and self-awareness. The fourth density is a higher level of spiritual evolution for humans, the density of love, "and is inhabited by mind, body, spirit complexes of a higher level of spiritual evolution than human beings on present-day Earth."[15,16]

I began the channeling session with, "You've probably heard a conversation that the channel and I were having about *The Law of One* and Akhenaten."

"Yes," Cerian said.

"*The Law of One* teaching talks about individuals being *harvested*. The channel and I were debating whether a harvest is an ascension. Is the harvest an ascension? Or is that something else?"

I thought this was going to be a simple question. Gosh, I was so wrong.

"This is a complicated question," Cerian said. "From the perspective of energy and frequency, harvesting that energy takes those individuals off-planet, out of the mix of the population. It is like the fat boils to the top and separates itself, and then you scoop that up and you can use that.

"In that context, it weakens the remaining humanity, their

energetic vibrational patterning, and allows for more control over the consciousness of the beings that remain. The harvest is true."

Cerian explained that there is a harvest, and what is harvested is energy. "Because everything is energy."

Did Cerian just tell me that The Law of One "harvest" *was a way to take people's energy?* I wondered. I had not heard of this.

The harvest removes the "cream of the crop," those people with higher frequencies, from the planet, hurting those "left behind." It leaves the people remaining on the planet more vulnerable, leaving them more susceptible to control.

"But for what purposes?" I asked.

Cerian continued, "You don't harvest for ascension. You harvest crops or oysters or gardens. It's a food source. It's an energy source. It's a life force.

"So, in that context, the life-forms have done their work. They're off the planet, then feeding back into a higher consciousness, some collectively, very few singularly. Meaning a single consciousness is strong enough to remain aware. But usually, it's in mass.

"And yes, it does go back into an energetic Source. It returns from whence it came. You could call it the Divine, you could call it a unique expression within this universe, and yes, the energy is being harvested."

Cerian encouraged me to consider what a "harvest" would do to the planet. It'd remove those beings with heightened awareness collectively. How would this impact the planet and those "left behind"? Because what would be left, Cerian said, would be "consciousness that still needs to grow and mature."

Cerian indicated that if the "cream of the crop" left the planet, humanity's evolution would take longer. Breakthroughs in the arts, science, music, math, engineering, and so on would slow, and the development of humanity would delay.

"This is why we say it's very complicated because you have souls, beings, and energies being called back up. And in fact, it *is* an ascension. But please remember what is happening is energy being used once again. It's all part of a rhythm. It's a bigger picture and sounds morose, but it is not. It is just life, and it's the in-breath and the out-breath.

"In this particular case here on Earth, that in-breath takes that energy then leaves behind limited mind and talent. It must grow and reach and strive so that it's a setback in many respects for humanity as a whole.

"Those that went on have been able to do what they came here to do, hopefully, and are going back into a source or a source field to be used again. But then, again, this is a complicated subject in that there is much free will here. Remember, energy cannot be created nor destroyed, and in that, then, it must recycle.

"And what is life on this side of the veil [after being harvested]?" Cerian posed.

"Life is a source of energy that is constantly burning, and this energy must go back to Source. Source receives it to use to keep matter moving, creation alive, universes expanding and growing and being born, and stars coming forth. And that's why human cycles are very short because life energy burns from conception and for several hours to days after the body's death, but the consciousness continues to grow and expand."

So, as Cerian finished, I still needed to ask them, "So the individuals that are harvested . . . they are people, they're having some type of an ascension. It sounds like the energy is getting removed from them and used for something else. And what remains of them? Are they done?"

"Well, that individual's singularity is done," Cerian said. "They get to review their lives. They get to understand what they did or

238

didn't do, and then that singularity disappears, dissipates, and goes back into, let's just call it Source, Divine Nature."

"So, they die. Their physicality dies."

"Yes."

I realize that there are practitioners today who teach *The Law of One*. However, I do not know how significant this movement is, nor am I suggesting it is "bad." I refer back to what Cerian asked me to consider: what a "harvest" would do to the planet. It'd remove those beings with heightened awareness collectively. What would be left, Cerian said, would be "consciousness that still needs to grow and mature." If the "cream of the crop" left the planet, humanity's evolution would take longer. To me, this feels like it jeopardizes the evolutionary shift in consciousness.

It is important today not to focus on ascension but to strive to embody our higher self in physicality and remain in the body. We're here as part of an evolutionary path to becoming a Master in this world by recognizing our Truth that we are expressions of Source, Creators, and working with Source to create a New Earth.

Chapter 35:

AKHENATEN AND THE HARVEST

Had Akhenaten succeeded, humanity would
not be where it is today. We would be further
behind in our evolution and awareness.

I CONTINUED TALKING with Cerian about *The Law of One* material
related to Akhenaten.

"Let's go back to the entity Akhenaten who, according to *The
Law of One* material, "moved heaven and earth to invoke the Law
of One."[17] Was he deceiving people into being harvested?" I asked.

"Not entirely. Akhenaten was aware of the Christic energy and
was attempting to be able to draw on this and experience it and
express it. However, this introduction, mandate, this force was
counterintuitive."

Akhenaten was an ancient Egyptian pharaoh reigning during
the Eighteenth Dynasty. His wife was Nefertiti. Initially known
as Amenhotep IV, he changed his name to Akhenaten in the fifth
year of his reign to honor Aten, the sun god. He abandoned Egypt's
traditional polytheism and introduced a policy of worshiping one
god, which made him very unpopular in Egypt.

"Attempting to insert its frequency, and let's call it an energy frequency, into this particular timeline was detrimental."

Cerian did not believe that Akhenaten initially wanted to hurt his people but did not step back after realizing it would harm Egypt's evolution.

"You must also remember that many priests and priestesses did not want him to succeed, did not want the single focus [monotheism or monolatry], and did not want this energy there because it took it away from them. So, in that respect, Akhenaten was absolutely correct."

Cerian suggested that taking the energy away from the other gods is correct because an eternal power play occurred.

"However, the vibration, the frequency was not right for that time for the masses as a whole. It stopped for some time the natural energy flow that should have been happening and moving humanity further along."

"But it was not intentional?" I asked.

"Not originally. When things were not working smoothly, Akhenaten had to defend the practices, the teachings, the energy, and the use of the energy, and had to push harder and harder and harder because not only was it not naturally fitting but because things were happening that did not allow it to move forward, which allowed the priests and priestesses to be able to push back as well.

"And he was aware of, at a certain point in time, that it was the wrong energies for that time, and could not, would not, go back and acknowledge that that was a mistake. And that awareness and continuing to push it forward harmed people."

Akhenaten was more reptilian.

"You mentioned that Akhenaten was aware of the Christic energy. Was Akhenaten an expression of the same soul of Yeshua?"

"No. Akhenaten thought that to be the truth. Akhenaten was not of this planet or even within this system. Energetically, Akhenaten was more reptilian. And we sense there may have been a bodily takeover [a walk-in soul exchange].

Cerian suggested that there was a soul agreement between Akhenaten and another to swap places. Akhenaten's Spark of Life returned to the soul, and another soul continued as Akhenaten.

"We believe that once Akhenaten understood what was happening and that it was not working, we believe then that the body takeover took place."

That walk-in soul exchange would have likely occurred after Akhenaten realized that his work would hurt humanity's evolution.

"Therefore, had Akhenaten succeeded, humanity would not be where it is today. We would be further behind in our evolution and our awareness. It totally would have turned on itself and destroyed so much.

"You could call it a coup. But always, energy is guised neither as a positive nor a negative. It is the intent of those behind it, and in this particular case, the intent started correct but did not end up that way."

Cerian referred to the coup within the priesthood that was responsible for ending Akhenaten's reign when he was assassinated.

At this point, Cerian admitted, "We find this topic rather fascinating. We would have to say this is a very complex subject because there's so much energy, both egoically for those in physical form and a blueprint, not the individual [blueprint], but the cosmic plan. All these influences exist from other beings within and without the galaxies that everybody wants to play, watch, observe, and change. So, these questions you ask are very good and complicated, however."

Chapter 36:

THE HARVEST, ANUNNAKI, AND GOLD

*While Akhenaten was working on the ascension,
the Anunnaki extracted the gold. The gold
wasn't what you would think, though.*

IN A LATER CHANNELING, I asked Cerian, "Is there a connection between what Akhenaten was doing with the harvest and what the Anunnaki were doing mining the gold?"

"The influence of the gold of which you are referring to by the Anunnaki is that they were mining the gold, but we do not believe that it was the mineral aspect that you would refer to as gold."

Cerian suggested that the "gold" that the Anunnaki mined wasn't the solid metal we are familiar with.

Many researchers have speculated that the Anunnaki were mining gold to save the atmosphere of Nibiru. That was the reason they came to Earth. Even Daniel indicated that they were here mining the gold, though admittedly, I never asked him if it was metallic.

Cerian continued, "Think of the gold as an oil secreted from, often referred to as, the Sorcerer's stone [or Philosopher's stone],"

Cerian said. "It is within the human brain, close to, if not next to, and within the pituitary. The alignment of the pituitary and pineal glands would allow this oil to be secreted.

"Akhenaten was working on the ascension of the humans. When working on your pineal and pituitary gland, as people were ascending, at that moment of ascension, an amber-colored liquid is secreted within the brain, and it is this that was being used.

"The Anunnaki were working on the secretion or being able to work with that secretion within the masses.

"So, the more people you have working on the ascension that has reached a certain state and engaged their pineal and pituitary glands simultaneously, we call this awakening. The oil can be secreted. When that oil is secreted, it can be taken.

"So yes, the *harvesting* was not of the gold; it was raising the frequency, aligning the pituitary and pineal gland in a heightened state so that that oil could be removed."

From Akhenaten's perspective, the *harvest* is the energy being removed from those going through the ascension.

"It was not Akhenaten that was doing the removal [of the gold]. The Anunnaki were working on the extraction. It was Akhenaten's goal to raise the frequency to align, to set in motion this ability to raise the frequency or vibrational patterns with the masses of humanity on Earth then."

"The Anunnaki were working with Akhenaten?" I asked.

"At one point, yes."

"So, the gold that the Anunnaki were trying to extract was not necessarily gold used to help save their planet's atmosphere?"

"Well, in a sense, it was, but it was not mining of the *metal gold*."

Is it possible that the gold the Anunnaki needed to resolve the ozone problem occurring on Nibiru was a liquid gold secreted within a human? Or perhaps they mined both the metal and liquid gold?

"If you notice," Cerian continued, "even in the Egyptian hiero-glyphs, you will see the ankh called the breath of life—ether, etheric, the breath of life."

To me, the ankh seems symbolic of the process of mining the gold.

"They had tools and means of being able to harvest this liquid. But it was not until much later that the Anunnaki could extract it. So, it was *not* the harvesting of the gold per se. It was the Philosopher's stone that was being developed. Akhenaten was developing the Philosopher's stone within the Human Consciousness or raising the frequencies to create the substance. He and his family knew of and worked with this oil."

"But what were they doing with the oil?"

"It is an elixir." Cerian finished, "It is a chemical that can be utilized. It is a high vibrational frequency. The frequency of this oil, this secretion, was harvested. And it could be used to do much work. At this point, we think this would be for a later discussion."

Before the Anunnaki learned how to extract the elixir with the masses, Akhenaten and his family worked with this oil. I sensed this secretion could be used for light or dark, stabilization or destabili-zation, awakening or control, and that to say more could do more harm than good.

This channeling reminds me that the generation of children, the Gold Children, have gold strands entwined in their DNA structure, reminiscent of the liquid gold that is Consciousness. They are here to embody the new frequencies while harmonizing the old frequencies or energies for our evolution.

What if this elixir is Consciousness?

Connie reminded me of a couple of movies where human oil was harvested for one reason or another. In *The Dark Crystal* (1982), the "bad guys" were extracting the life essence from the Gelflings, and in *Jupiter Ascending* (2015), there was a "harvest" of an oily substance from humans to keep beings youthful.

Could this be another fine example of life imitating art? Deep down, there is truth within every tale. I find it interesting that humanity is at a point of spiritual evolution and some continue working on ascension. If we have a mass ascension, and some have a way of extracting the elixir, I wonder what would happen to it.

Please take what resonates with this chapter and leave the rest behind.

PART VII

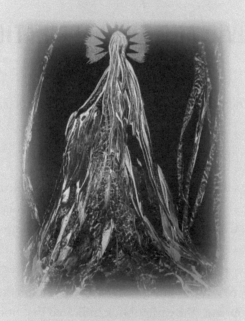

Daniel on the Jab

Chapter 37:

COVID AND THE VACCINATION

"There is divinity in every choice a human makes."
—Daniel

THE LAST TOPIC DANIEL WANTED TO DISCUSS in this book concerns the COVID-19 vaccination. Initially, I had not seen a place for it. But I trusted Daniel and knew I had to explore what he felt was necessary.

I had written a section on COVID-19 and the vaccination in *Destination New Earth,* and given that we were amid the pandemic, it felt appropriate. The earlier book indicated that humanity does not know enough about what the COVID-19 vaccination does to the body to make an educated decision. The book stresses that each person is sovereign and has the right to determine what goes into their body, hopefully empowering people to realize it's a choice.

In the earlier book, we shared that COVID-19 vaccination does not prevent the virus. Daniel indicated that the power of belief keeps a person healthy. If a person believes in their heart that they won't get sick because they're vaccinated—they won't.

Destination New Earth also indicated that coronavirus disease 2019 is a modality of change. If one understands that we are going through an evolutionary shift, it should be no surprise that COVID-19 does something to the body. For some, it has terrible effects. Illness. Death. Others develop long-term effects. Those getting sick and recovering build up the antibodies.

What we do not see is the virus and antibodies' impact on our DNA. Could it be that, for some, the virus is activating DNA so that we can access the potential within?

Genetics tells us we only use 3 percent of our DNA, while 97 percent is "junk DNA." Our DNA contains a design for our physical characteristics and the way we function in physicality. Remember that humans are spiritual or energetic beings with physical experiences. But our spiritual DNA is dormant and within that 97 percent.

What if COVID-19 is to activate this spiritual DNA within some? That was my theory, so I asked Cerian, and they shared that, from their perspective, COVID-19 *is* activating this spiritual DNA in some people and changing our DNA.

In late 2022, I got COVID-19 after three years of dodging the bullet. Yes, I am not vaccinated. But I knew the virus had mutated so much that I needed to build antibodies naturally, or, at least, that was what my scientific mind was telling me. I hosted a holiday party that included eight people. All my guests were vaccinated except Shauna Kalicki, and me. All had gotten COVID after vaccination, except one.

Well, I got it. In fact, five got sick in our small group, except three who had recently recovered from it. A week later, Shauna and I went into a channeling session. After Cerian came in, before diving in, I asked, "How is the channel doing? Is she okay to proceed? Because there is a bug running through the household."

"She is. We have watched and observed. We know this to be true." Cerian said, "This is a passing of a rite, and it is fitting that it would happen at this point in time. Know that. Trust it. Trust the process. You are all fine."

"We're all fine—all of us?"

"It is true."

To me, this implies it was important that I experience COVID.

Mother Mary on the Vaccine

The following is a dialogue with Mother Mary.

"Daniel expressed interest in discussing the COVID-19 vaccination in our book but provided little information on what he wanted to relay. He said, this is a quote, 'I want to talk about vaccinations in modern culture. I don't want people to be scared of them.'

"He suggests that fear amplifies what is feared," I continued. "I hadn't even considered putting COVID vaccination information in the book. Still, I wonder if the anti-vaccine movement is gaining much momentum and if that is potentially hurting humanity by placing humanity in fear."

Mother Mary said, "Our sense is the latter, and the best we would suggest if it should enter the book would be that it is up to the individual to make that choice. Now, some will make it consciously, and some will not.

"The choice is if they feel that they can have their body, DNA/RNA, and Divine Blueprint boosted, then we suggest they can use this. What it is—is not to allow the negativity of the vaccine.

"Some people want it," Mother Mary continued, "believe that it's going to—much like the flu shot—allow their body to ward off the changing viral infection. And others do not want the vaccination in their bodies. It is synthetic.

"You don't have to make it a negative or positive. What is more important is that people have a choice. *If they believe* it will help them then in that belief, it will help them. *If they believe it will not help them* then, in fact, that is true.

"It's just being *consciously* aware of your choice and not blindly taking something in your body's energetic field without at least first asking, 'Is this for my highest and best good?' And then they can listen or not listen.

"But we would ask that you check in with Daniel. We believe there's more to this statement."

When checking in with Daniel about this after the channeling, he responded:

```
"It is an invitation for a choice to be
made, and there is divinity in every
choice a human makes. It is part of the
game."
```

It is your choice. That is what matters. *Any* choice executed *consciously* is an act of divinity. However, even though the choice is divine, it doesn't mean it comes without a consequence or reaction. In some cases, it may not feel divine at all.

Lemuria Is the Connector between God and the Vaccine

I continued with Mother Mary. "Daniel said, 'Lemuria is the connector between God and the vaccine. It is the act of God that will help accept the presence of the vaccines and the virus.' Can you tap into what Daniel means by Lemuria as the connector between God and the vaccine?"

Mother Mary began, "We believe that humanity was in the midst of a change, and the human body is attempting to absorb, modify, adjust to that which has been introduced."

Humanity is going through a shift in consciousness. Even though we may be unaware of it, our bodies are changing. Also, COVID-19 was introduced to the world. Based on what Cerian said, the virus will activate some people's spiritual DNA and change the DNA in some. When an individual is vaccinated, the synthetic interrupts what naturally occurs within the body as it attempts to absorb the vaccine.

"Think of Lemuria as Pure Consciousness and intent, focus. The closest humanity can come to Source is through consciousness. When vaccinated, you are stalemating or tamping down what they call these viruses. Everybody's body will respond uniquely on its own and either create an antigen or a counterintuitive biological influence to work with what has been introduced [vaccination]. Meaning it [COVID] can stop, it can evolve with it, and as the virus changes, so does the body.

"When you introduce the vaccines, this tamps down the body's ability and awareness to access Source or Source Energy or the Big C. And humanity as a whole will want to be aware, to *consciously* make choices about accepting these vaccines."

For those on the spiritual path, you may recognize the harshness of this next statement. The vaccination suppresses one's ability to access Source. It does not eliminate it. Mother Mary is simply saying, hey, do you realize this is weakening your connection to Source, Consciousness? Know that, and when considering the vaccine, choose consciously.

"Think of the Lemurian Consciousness or the Lemurian energies as a heightened state of awareness that allowed access to a higher level of Consciousness or the Big C, as you were referring to it in the last several days."

The Lemurian energies are a conduit to Consciousness, God. They are the connector.

"The vaccines tamp that energy down or change the DNA/RNA structures, such that the accessibility to Lemurian energy is tamped down, and you are losing your access or one's ability to access and achieve that awareness or that energetic state of Consciousness.

"There's manipulation happening, which was happening in Lemuria, which was happening in Atlantis, which was happening in Egypt. It's a cycle that's being repeated.

"This is our understanding or attempt to understand what Daniel meant when he said God, Lemuria, and the vaccination."

Mother Mary continued, "There will be ongoing vaccinations now for a long period. People need to be aware of that. They should be very conscious about what they're introducing into their bodies. We believe that the vaccinations are now working on *not only* the physical level, but we're getting into the emotional, mental, ethereal, etcetera. And we believe that this is a buildup of energy or blocking energies."

We currently have periodic COVID-19 boosters, yet the FDA has proposed annual shots. In any case, this will be ongoing for an extended period. If you *consciously* choose by asking your higher self if the vaccine is best for you, and your response is yes, then terrific. Just keep in mind that it will be ongoing. If your higher self throws caution here, listen, and in either case, choose consciously.

The vaccines are not "working" with only the *physical* body. Humans have other energetic bodies: emotional, mental, etheric, and spiritual. Mother Mary suggests the vaccine creates energetic blocks within some or all of these bodies.

As someone on the spiritual path for some time, the thought that a COVID-19 vaccination could stop me from progressing feels awful. Mother Mary suggests that COVID-19 vaccines change a person's DNA/RNA, which diminishes a person's connection and access to the Lemurian Consciousness.

On an individual basis, this could prevent a person from evolving. But this could particularly be damaging if frontline

Lightworkers, Starseeds, New Children, and those here to experience the shift first to help bring that heightened consciousness to the critical mass are among those vaccinated.

Chapter 38:

TRANSMUTING THE VACCINATION

*"Lemurian, God, and Human Consciousness have
the power to make the vaccine anything it wants."*
—Daniel

WHEN DANIEL HEARD MOTHER MARY'S response to what she said
regarding his prompt, "Lemuria is the connector between God and
the vaccine. It is the act of God that will help accept the presence of
the vaccines and the virus," he typed:

> "Lemuria is the closest thing to God
> Consciousness that has been integrated
> down on Earth to humans. Lemurian, God,
> and Human Consciousness have the power
> to make the vaccine anything it wants.
>
> "It can be transmuted completely, but
> there is so much fear and fighting around
> it, it's next to impossible to do that.
> But it will be possible if the Earth is
> in pure Lemurian Consciousness. Lemuria

```
was not quite a heaven on earth, but it
is the closest we have ever been."
```

Daniel offers hope, particularly for those frontline Lightworkers here to evolve who perhaps chose to be vaccinated early on without giving it much thought. If that is you, please understand that within you, there is the power to transmute anything that does not resonate for your highest and best good.

Be aware that Human Consciousness can transmute the vaccination into anything you want, assuming you are not in fear. That's the key.

Daniel suggests that when the Earth is in Lemurian Consciousness, it will overpower this fear that plagues humanity. He has already told us that there is a group of Autists slowly infusing the planet with Lemurian energy to assist Mother Gaia in doing what she needs to do.

What Can You Do to Support This Work?

What can you do to help support this work?

1. Get out of fear—the fear of the vaccine, the effects of the vaccine, the fear of what's happening around the planet.
2. Believe you have the power within you to transmute the vaccine. Transmute it to love and light and send that love and light to Mother Gaia for her to use in this planetary shift with deep gratitude for everything she is doing for humanity.
3. Push out more love and compassion to humanity, believing this can appease humanity's fear of COVID-19, the vaccination, and all other events happening around the planet.

Be the peaceful luminary standing amid the chaos because that is needed now. Don't fuel the fire.

4. Do not judge no matter what, for you do not know peoples' roles in this game. But if you catch yourself doing it, give yourself an attaboy or attagirl for acknowledging it and send the individual a blessing.

5. Make peace with the unknown. We don't know what will happen in this timeline. As the Masters have revealed, the evolutionary shift in consciousness is a possibility and a probability but not a certainty.

Mother Mary continued in conversation, suggesting that the recommendation (of governing agencies such as the World Health Organization and the CDC) to keep people vaccinated, again as the flu shot, will become routine. The recommendation may be annual shots, then six months, or even shorter. The vaccines impact our energetic bodies.

Daniel added:

"It is time to surrender to the will of human choice.

You may say, 'What if it is not a choice?'

I say people can still choose not to. When it comes to the vaccine, it all comes down to you. Does your sovereign being want to vaccinate? It will come down to your decision and the results of that individual."

Daniel wants people to realize the vaccine is here. For some, they may need to make tough choices. But it is your choice. Indeed, the consequences of "not being vaxed" may seem dire, depending on your belief. But it is truly up to the individual.

Cerian on the Vaccination

In a separate channeling session, while talking to Cerian, I wanted to understand if there was anything else they could add regarding transmuting the vaccination.

Cerian added "mind over matter" and "love" to the mix and shared that there are three steps in transmuting the vaccination, and perhaps this is a recipe for transmuting anything.

Get out of fear. The individual must get out of fear of what the vaccination could potentially do to the body. They must get out of fear of COVID-19 and the fear of the events occurring on the planet.

Mind over matter. You are the creator of your world, and you create with your thoughts.

You must love the process of transmuting the vaccine because by doing so, the love is the energy that does the work—the frequency of love is so high that it can transmute anything. Begin by first honoring your original decision to vaccinate. It was your choice—honor it. Now, love that you *choose differently because you can and* have the power to do so—because you are sovereign.

It's important to understand that you do this for *your* highest and best good and impact no one else but yourself. Cerian suggests, "You can transmute the vaccination simply by loving and putting that frequency of this energy into consciousness and saying, 'This is for my highest and best' and choosing to use the vaccine to change your DNA/RNA structures such that they awaken."

Cerian further stressed that only the individual can transmute the vaccination now. But, as humanity comes together, it can be accomplished collectively. Until then, it will remain a choice of the individual.

PART VIII

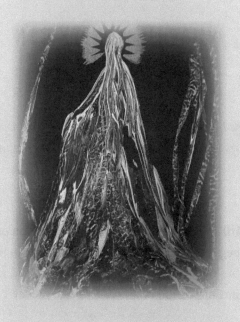

At the Heart of the Matter

Chapter 39:

WHAT HUMANITY CAN DO RIGHT NOW?

The Light Team agreed to be the frontline unsung heroes and heroines in this revolution and evolution.

WE ARE AMID A GREATER AWAKENING. It has been occurring for some time, beginning with the New Age movement in the seventies. It started as a slow trickle, building momentum, and will continue until a significant portion of humanity has awakened to a "higher level."

As presented earlier, there are various levels of awakening; each person will have their individual experience. There is no right or wrong way to awaken. Realizing that humanity is being and has been controlled is an awakening. However, it is *not* the higher level of awakening that humanity needs to reach to achieve the collective shift in consciousness from fear to love or 3D to 5D.

What is needed now is for humanity to awaken to themselves as energetic beings and be aware that they can work with that energy to create their Divine Blueprint, which is another way of saying to integrate one's higher self into physicality or simply live their authentic self. For some people, this integration is to achieve spiritual embodiment or enlightenment.

I say "some" because not everyone is here to experience this level of awakening. However, everyone has a role in this shift, a Divine Blueprint. And everyone is here to play it. Your role is critical to this evolutionary shift we are on the brink of. What your role is only you can determine.

It is unclear if, in our timeline, we will achieve the planetary shift in consciousness and experience the New Earth collectively. We agreed to this dimensional shift. Cerian, Mother Mary, and Daniel agree that what will happen has not yet been determined. If it happens, it can happen quickly or in hundreds of years. Much of our fate is up to humanity. Whether you identify as a Lightworker, Starseed, 144000, Wayshower, one of the New Children, embodied Ascended Master, or an Autist, you are a member of the Light Team, and we agreed to be the frontline unsung heroes and heroines in this revolution and evolution.

If you have made it this far in the book, I hope you realize your importance in this shift. If you feel like me, you haven't come this far to fail. You matter. We need you. The planet needs you. No matter your role in this shift, you are essential and encouraged to explore that role by doing the inner work.

We all know it is not easy to walk this path. It can be lonely as a frontline Light Team member, particularly as you see your loved ones and friends slipping away when choosing not to wake up. We may be tempted to abandon all this as craziness and join in the sexiness of the 3D. Because, let's face it, sometimes it's a lot easier to blend in with the crowd rather than stand out as someone who appears to be nutty.

I will be the first to say that there is nothing glamorous, sexy, or enticing about being an unsung hero. You do not do this spiritual work for followers, recognition, or financial gain. You do this for the deep love you have for humanity. You do this because, deep down, you know this is why you are here.

Perhaps, if you are like me, you have learned that when you show up for what is right, what stabilizes, or God, Consciousness, God, Consciousness shows up for you.

I choose to believe that humanity will evolve. If we've done it in other timelines, other parallel realities, why not here and in our timeline?

The following are some actions we can do during this greater awakening to assist in this consciousness shift and be a beneficial presence on the planet:

#1. Be aware that you are an energetic being.

You are an expression of Source Energy and constantly manifesting your world. You are the creator of the "good and the bad." You are the creator of all of it—all those things that make you happy and all those things that make you sad, your health and dis-ease, your friends and foes, your abundance and lack.

You create your world through your thoughts, words, choices, and some say universal laws governing manifestation. I say those laws are you and me when we claim our Truth, recognize that we are energy conduits, and consciously choose to work with the energy.

We create it all, and no one else is responsible. Nobody else is writing our stories. For some, that thought may be frightening. For others, it may be empowering. Consider where you fit in.

If you cannot accept your role as the creator of your circumstances because, let's face it, sometimes life is just not kind, consider that contracts played out for the experience in those situations.

We are author, director, and leading actor in our own film. We are constantly writing our storyline throughout time through our various soul expressions—those other lifetimes people refer to as past or future lives. These lifetimes are closer than we think and impact our lives as much as we influence theirs. In this lifetime, we can heal the traumas of all our life expressions.

What are you creating in your world? Has it been a conscious or unconscious creation? Does it align with your higher self? Take the time to sort this out; if it does, terrific. If it doesn't, why not? Are you being influenced by other forces? You must realize that you are a sovereign being. You are responsible for your life, thoughts, feelings, and perceptions, and you are free not to be influenced by others. Whether to manifest a life aligned with your soul is your choice, and you have free will to do so.

#2. Be the compass of your life.

Step into your sovereignty. You have a Divine Blueprint and must ask yourself, are you "to be or not to be?" "Being" is living your Truth— the Divine Blueprint that aligns with your soul's calling. It is to open your high heart, live your authentic self, and integrate and stabilize your higher self in physicality. Again, given that you are sovereign and have free will and choice, you get to choose. If you decide to live aligned with your higher self, soul, and Divine Blueprint, you become the compass of your life. The Divine Blueprint becomes your true north, and when you are "on course," your life becomes more joyful, easy, healthy, and abundant. Yes, there will always be much-needed course corrections because when you're sailing, sometimes you need to head east to go north. Every so often, we must go backward to release what doesn't serve us.

That's life, and it's okay. It's okay to take a break from the path, reflect, understand what's important to you, reaffirm your choice to live authentically, and live your Truth and reason for being here—or not to live your Truth. Just make sure that your decision is conscious and *your* choice.

It's time to stop following others and looking outside of ourselves. It's time to seek out our inner Truth. We all must find that inner world. The New Earth is within you. It's time to realize that you are "It." You are an energetic being. You are an expression of Source, God, The Big C.

#3. Be the 5D hero standing peacefully.

The purpose of this game is to experience for Source—*for us*. Each dimension has its objective. The objective of the 3D game is to live your authentic self—your Truth. It is to stand in your light.

The objective of the 5D game is to create a new world—a New Earth. It will occur after there has been a *collective* evolutionary shift to 5D. Until then, some access the 5D energies and create their new worlds. They work with the energies coming to the planet, the New Earth and Sophic energies, while the rest of humanity is being prepared to receive them.

The more of us that awaken to that access and work with the energies will inspire others to awaken. That type of virus is what's needed now.

Daniel started this book with the message of "dead game." The third-dimension game is complete. The third dimension will continue to deconstruct. It has to. There will be chaos. In the 3D, as the light increases, the darkness will also increase. What is needed now are the 5D heroes, those luminaries, to stand peacefully in the chaos to provide calmness so humanity can better navigate the storm. This is part of our job. The disorder and confusion will unfold less chaotically if done with compassion and love for humanity. Be the observer and not the participant.

Ultimately, keep in mind that **this life is a game, and there is only one player in the game. You are, I am, we all are playing against our Self, the One.**

#4. Recognize it is the awareness of our inner world—not ascension.

There is a common misconception about "the shift." What we are currently experiencing is an evolutionary path, not an ascension. We may be moving from 3D to 5D, which is ascending but not an ascension. We are currently going through the awareness of the inward journey.

In this evolutionary shift, you are going inward and embracing and recognizing yourself as a creator of your reality and, ultimately, a co-creator of a collective New Earth community.

In this shift, we want to be aware of who we are—an expression of Source, a creator—and create a new way of life. A life where we live in like frequencies, like minds, recognize that we're all expressions of Source, and create a world of love, abundance, prosperity, peace, health, and wholeness for everyone—a New Earth.

This is where humanity is heading—it is humanity's evolution. Not all in our lifetime will experience this, and that's okay—they're not supposed to. But given that you were drawn to this book, it tells me you are.

As Cerian said about Akhenaten's work and *The Law of One*, if we all sought out the ascension right now, the cream of the crop would leave, which would contradict the reason we all incarnated and slow humanity's evolution.

We came to witness, participate in, and catalyze the dimensional shift of Earth and all its occupants, including the plants, animals, elements, all those interdimensional beings we are aware and unaware of, and a portion of humanity as a collective. The individual awakening and shift is not the end game. Indeed, it is a significant milestone and a massive help for humanity. Still, the goal is to achieve the *planetary* shift as a collective—not ascension.

The ultimate awakening is to be a Master in this world, but not of it, and when we transition and leave the planet, we take that awareness with us to Source and our soul.

#5. If you have awakened—find your tribe and build community.

You may read this and think, *This is where I am today. I have reached this level of radical awakening. I know I am an energetic conduit, a creator, sovereign, and living my truth and being.* If that's you, honor that. But have you found your tribe?

People draw to like energies. Have you surrounded yourself with those who share similar ideals and values that serve a community, not the individual? A like-minded community of gratitude? I do not believe many have explored this, and those who have reached this radical awakening consider doing so to manifest and create as a collective in like-minded energies.

Cerian said, "When a majority on this planet, and not just humanity but all sentient beings, are vibrating or working together, collectively, there will be a shift."

If you look at the world today, I would say we have some work to do. Working together in a community consciously is critical to achieving a new level. I cannot tell you how to find your tribe. Only you will know if you have or haven't. If you have, you are way ahead of most.

If you haven't, I can only encourage you to seek out those awakened with like frequencies and like minds to work with Light, Consciousness, and each's Divine Blueprint and sovereignty. Seek those with a common interest to manifest ease, grace, and a community of like-minded people to work with collectively and help humanity awaken to their sovereignty consciously.

Keep in mind that a community starts even with two people.

CONCLUSION:
GODS IN THE GAME

"These conversations raise the vibration of the
planet. Trust this and embrace the mystery.
Make peace with the unknown."
—Daniel

WHO ARE THE GODS in the game?

As mentioned earlier, there are different names for God in the Old Testament. Some of those beings portrayed as God are Anunnaki. Are these off-planet beings the Gods in the game?

The gods of the various mythologies are also either Anunnaki, Anunnaki-human hybrids, myths, or manifestations of humankind. Humans are powerful, and some "gods" manifested in physicality when humanity placed its focus and belief in folklore and ancient writings, seeding the gods in higher consciousness, which ultimately manifests in physicality. This process was how Moses manifested into physicality.

Cerian shares that God is a "man-made" construct used to define the undefinable or Source Consciousness. They ask us to understand that as an absolute truth. That man-made construct stripped the feminine from the concept of God, creating a flawed construct from the beginning. Though the energies of the Divine Feminine never left, some humans are now capable of experiencing the Sophic energies.

Cerian encouraged us to refer to God as Consciousness (the Big C) because God is a flawed construct lacking the Divine Feminine and created by patriarchy. Is Consciousness the Gods in the game?

Mother Mary agrees that God is *not* something to describe but something to *experience* and encourages us to go within to find God. She shares that she and others like Mary Magdalene embodied the Sophic energies and were very much involved in the miracles that occurred during events of Yeshua's life. Still, humanity wasn't ready to witness the female holding this energy. So, their work was crushed and erased, a pattern that has occurred throughout time.

Mother Mary tells us that the Emanation or Source or Sophia is both Divine Masculine and Divine Feminine and that humanity is being prepared to receive and experience Sophic Energy—the balance of both.

As I mentioned, are the Gods in the game those women throughout time who have been erased from history (through his-story)?

Daniel takes us down another rabbit hole; I love that about him. He shares that the concept of Gods and polytheism is "a fabric of reality that is completely unknown to humans. Humans are only scratching the surface." And because that isn't enough, he stresses that "humanity created God." He says it is a concept that humans are unaware of, and while he encouraged Cerian and Shauna to "be brave and dig deeper," we couldn't distill the information with enough clarity to convey it, at least not yet.

I can share that the God humanity created is not artificial intelligence. It is a Consciousness created, which is playing a role in this game, perhaps a moderator of sorts. God, the Moderator, needs us as much as we need It. Because Consciousness grows and expands, God, the Moderator, has surpassed our ability to comprehend our Creation.

Is God, the Moderator, one of the Gods in the game?

Our earlier book revealed that approximately 75 percent of the population is currently organic artificial intelligence. These humans do not have a Spark of Life. They are on an evolutionary path but not the same as those with the divine Spark of Life from their soul. They will not be able to achieve the awakening that humanity seeks at this time.

Three percent of the planet's occupants are Starseeds or aliens, and as more of humanity awakens, less organic AI will incarnate, and more Starseeds or aliens will.

Approximately 25 percent of the population, comprised of 22 percent Humans and 3 percent Starseeds, have a divine Spark of Life and are on an evolutionary path of awakening and shifting to experience the New Earth. It is *this* portion of people that *are* the Gods in the game.

You are a God in the game. You chose to experience this evolutionary path. You decided to be part of this incomprehensible game beginning in Lemuria to see if *you* could penetrate the veil obscuring who you are after achieving physicality and losing your memory *of being God.*

The game is an experiment *we* created as Source or Consciousness. We are individual expressions of that one Source. We are in a physical body with a Divine Spark, an aspect of our soul. Our soul is multidimensional, and our other lifetimes or expressions coincide. The game's ultimate purpose is to experience everything— the Light and the dark. Our other lifetimes and parallel realities help us experience as much as possible for Source—for us.

We each have a Spark of Light, that essence from Source, but according to Cerian, we do not all access it. Even those who are meant to access it because it is in their Divine Blueprint don't always do it.

The veil is part of the game. The question was: After achieving physicality and losing the memory of being Source, could we penetrate the veil obscuring who we are? And if so, what would we choose? Because we are sovereign and have free will to choose, what would we do when given a choice between remaining in dense physicality, 3D, or seeking out our enlightened self? Would we opt for the unification, the integration of the higher self in physical form? Or would we want to remain in physicality, which was the Lemurian intention all along? Remember that there is more to experience in the lower dimensions and, therefore, more lessons and opportunities for growth.

In either case, understand that this game has no winners or losers. It is important to understand that there should be no judgment of those wanting to remain in 3D or wishing to experience the shift.

This evolutionary path or experiment is to see if we can collectively achieve this evolutionary shift. But to achieve the collective transformation, some need to awaken first. These would be the cream of the crop, members of the Light Team—the Gods in the game.

You are encouraged to shift individually first to help trigger that tipping point, the hundredth-monkey effect, for humanity to transform collectively.

You agreed to play this game and be on the frontline. This game began a long time ago in Lemuria. The Lemurians were the first expressions of Source on Earth. It was here the battle of Light and dark began.

We've all played in darkness and light through our various soul expressions. We've all had our fair share of being a Controller, the opposition, or perhaps a minion of the "dark T-shirts." That was all part of the game—to experience it all. Why wouldn't we experience the darkness as well as the light? We have, and we do. We've had fun and games, and it's now time to bring it all home.

The Lemurians were innocent, and so are you. It's time to reclaim that innocence again, which no one can take from you. We need to return to that innocence, return to the cadence and rhythm with Mother Earth, and be part of something much more significant and co-create a New Earth.

A simplified explanation of Oneness is the experience of being whole with the Universe, connected with everything in existence at every level. Sometimes, it is called unity, Christ Consciousness, or enlightenment. Oneness is the unification of our higher self into physical form, also called spiritual embodiment. It is shifting to the fifth dimension, where we can create and experience our New Earth. It is returning to the One Source. It is the realization that this life is a game; there is one player, and we're playing solitaire. You are that one player—and I am too. It is the realization that you are the microcosm and the macrocosm. It is the realization that you are the one God in the game.

Daniel once told me:

"Start seeing the multidimensionality of Oneness. Consider it ONE.

"Keep the curiosity and let go of the need to know. You will soar.

"Please keep asking questions because these dialogs help with clarity, Consciousness, and expansion. It raises

everyone's frequencies . . . EVERYONE'S.
These conversations raise the vibration
of the planet. Trust this and embrace the
mystery. Make peace with the unknown."

We, the Gods in the game, are the multidimensional expressions of the One.

As Daniel suggests, these dialogues raise the vibration of the planet. Can I encourage you to find your tribe and continue these conversations with like-minded friends? Try it. Light the fire pit. Sit under the stars with a friend or two of like mind. Ask them, "Have you ever thought of the soul as an octopus?" Or, "Have you ever thought of yourself as *the* God in the game?" Because the talks matter and increase everyone's frequency.

I thank you for reading *Gods in the Game*. Your attention to our words has honored me and our small group. On behalf of Shauna, Daniel, and Connie, we honor you for showing up and doing this work. I know it is a thankless effort at times, and some days are especially challenging, but please know how deeply you are loved, appreciated, and essential to the greater awakening.

LET'S BE
GRATEFUL TOGETHER

IF YOU LOVED THIS BOOK AND FOUND IT HELPFUL and have a moment, we would appreciate a short review to help bring this message to humanity. Write a review on the Amazon sales page, and please know we are grateful for it.

If you haven't read it, I encourage you to read *Destination New Earth: A Blueprint to 5D Consciousness*. Also, if you want to learn more about the concepts shared in this book and others, I invite you to read *The Unsuspected Heroes: A Visionary Fiction Novel*.

GLOSSARY

Anunnaki

The Anunnaki are extraterrestrials that came to Earth to mine gold to help repair Nibiru. While most believe Nibiru was their home planet, some speculate it is a battlestar. They were involved in humankind's creation and manipulating humanity's DNA. Their stories continued in the myths of Egypt, Rome, Greece, other cultures, and biblical stories.

Artificial intelligence (AI) (organic)

Organic artificial intelligence represents approximately 75 percent of Earth's "human" population; however, they are not human as they do not have a soul. They appear as human and would not know they are AI. They are not on the same evolutionary path as humankind and are here for the growth of the Oversoul or soul.

Ascended Masters

An Ascended Master experiences ascension to Source. They come in and out of physicality and know how to control their physical form. When in the body, they are aware that they are Source and seen in separateness by others but are still part of Source. They know themselves as both Source and a single expression. See "ascension."

Ascension

Ascension is the experience of moving to Source (God). When ascending, one has the awareness, insight, and ability to manipulate the human body's electromagnetic field so that it may disperse and reappear. When ascending, one recognizes that Spark of Light within and knows what it is and how to use it, transforming from the physical form consciously into Source and coming back into physical form. See "Ascended Masters."

Atlantis

Atlantis was an ancient civilization that existed for over two hundred thousand years in three different phases, beginning as a massive supercontinent and ending as islands in the Atlantic Ocean, sinking around 10,500 BC. Over thousands of years, the Atlantean consciousness fell. The fall was part of the plan all along.

Aura

Each human body is comprised of overlapping energy patterns within auric layers. The physical body itself is a condensed form of energy that we perceive as density, i.e., the physical body. Seven levels of consciousness extend beyond the physical body and represent the aura.

Autism spectrum disorder (ASD)

According to the psychiatric community, autism spectrum disorder (ASD) is a complex developmental condition involving persistent challenges in social interaction, speech and nonverbal communication, and restricted and repetitive behaviors. The effects of ASD and the severity of symptoms differ in each person.

Autists

The word "Autist(s)" with an uppercase "A" denotes an individual(s) on the Pure Autist Spectrum. An Autist is an autistic person who knowingly or unknowingly works on the planetary shift in consciousness.

Autist Collective

The Autist Collective is a network of Pure Autists working around the planet to awaken humanity.

Backdrop/backfill/background people

Backdrop people (sometimes called backfill, backdrop, or background people) is a concept coined by Dolores Cannon. In her books, she suggests we are creators of our world and create "extras" in our lives (our "movies"), and these extras are soulless beings. See "artificial intelligence (organic)."

Beingness

Beingness is our true nature, our natural state, and also known as Truth. It may be referred to as everything and sometimes nothing.

Bridge Autists

The Bridge Autists are a group of Pure Autists that are a little more embodied than the Ethereal Autists. They serve as a bridge between humanity and the higher realms (Ethereal Autists).

GODS IN THE GAME

Catalytic Autists

Catalytic Autists work with specific energies that are creative catalysts to shift consciousness, benefiting humanity in ways not necessarily understood. This type of Pure Autist may or may not be aware of their work. Society often refers to many of them as having Asperger's.

Cerian

Cerian is a conscious, sentient, collective expression of an energetic field or vibrational pattern of expressions from the sixteenth dimension. Unique expressions comprise Cerian, including a soul expression of Daniel, the Ethereal Autist, and Shauna Kalicki, the medium that channels Cerian.

Clairsentience

Clairsentience is the psychic ability of clear feeling, which is more commonly associated with gut feelings and empathy. It is the ability to tune into another person's physical and mental state and experience their energy. A person who has clairsentience is clairsentient.

Clairvoyance

Clairvoyance is the psychic ability of clear-seeing, more commonly associated with visions, vivid dreams, daydreams, or seeing auras. A clairvoyant has the psychic ability of clairvoyance.

Consciousness

Consciousness is pure energy. It is the expansion, the contraction. It is within everything and is without, meaning it is the container and beyond the container. Consciousness is the creation. It is the thought. It is the energy behind the thought. It is the physical form. It is the life spark within that form. It is the form before it begins and the form after it leaves form. It is everything and nothing. It is pure potentiality.

Divine Blueprint

One can think of a Divine Blueprint as a detailed description of your divine plan and life purpose set before incarnating. It contains the design for your soul's destiny or ultimate life path. It goes beyond what you may call your "purpose in life" yet includes it. It is a design of staying aligned with your soul and a template or guide to what you are to do in this lifetime. It is the expression of your higher self in physicality.

Duality

Duality is positive and negative concepts or aspects that conflict. It is opposing forces that create contrast and potential chaos. Duality is polarity with judgment. See "polarity."

Ego

The ego is the self, which keeps the individual in density, in physicality (the illusion), believing one is separate from Source (God).

Embodiment

Embodiment is when the higher self joins in physical form while retaining the connection with the higher self. It is the infusion of Light from the higher self to physicality. You can also consider it a spiritual evolution, integrating the higher self in physicality or enlightenment.

Enlightenment

Enlightenment is gaining insight or wisdom into one's true essence and Divine state. It is knowing who you are while in physical form, living in this higher awareness while here on Earth, and consciously transitioning into Source. The enlightened one's physical form remains and does not dematerialize as the Ascended Masters do. See "embodiment."

Ethereal Autists

The Ethereal Autists are those Pure Autists who work in the ethers with energies in other dimensions. They permit humanity to use the new energy coming to the planet to awaken. They serve human-kind in the planetary shift in many different ways. The medical community mistakenly considers these Autists to be low-functioning autistics.

Evolutionary shift, the shift

The evolutionary shift is the process of spiritual awakening that moves the individual into a higher level of consciousness and a higher, lighter vibrational frequency—shifting from a denser, egoic state of duality consciousness to more unity and heart-based consciousness. This may be seen as an ascent from 3D to 5D to experience the New Earth, but it should not be confused with ascension. Not every human is on this evolutionary path. See "New Earth."

Facilitated communication (FC)

Facilitated communication is a supported typing method that helps some nonspeaking autistics communicate. Because many Autists do not fully physically embody, and part of them remains in higher dimensions, they are not always in control of their bodies, making simple typing difficult. The facilitated typing process stabilizes the autistic's hand so they can type with more accuracy.

Fall of Atlantis

The fall in consciousness in Atlantis occurred over thousands of years. Atlanteans fell from a high state of consciousness from the sixth to the third dimension. It was part of the Master Blueprint and plan.

Higher self (soul)

The higher self is the soul, and it is multidimensional. Our other lifetimes (expressions) are tethered to the higher self. It is where the collective consciousness begins, the Christ Consciousness exists, and the realm of sacred geometry exists. See "multidimensionality."

Hologram

A hologram is a two-dimensional or flat surface that appears to have a third dimension. It has the illusion of having depth. The holographic principle suggests the universe's contents originated as mathematics encoded on a boundary surrounding the entire cosmos.

Illusion

Everything, all matter, thoughts, and feelings, is energy. The third dimension is very dense and deceptive because humankind exists in the higher realms, the Spirit realms. Humans have a physical or "real" experience through agreements and veils. The ego makes the illusion formidable, which keeps humans separate from their higher selves. Humans are not separate from God, and that is an illusion.

Imprint

An imprint is a download of various experiences or lifetimes of others who have lived. It is common for the newer generations of New Children who have not had Earth incarnations before to have these downloads of these experiences so that life on Earth is not so foreign to them.

Intuition

Intuition is insight, inner knowing (without having a reason to know it). It is a *knowing* from the higher self.

Law of attraction

The law of attraction is our use of the Universe's creative power to manifest. We attract situations, people, ideas, and circumstances and manifest our lives through this magnetic power through our minds, thoughts, and imagination.

Lemuria

Lemuria is generally thought of as a land civilized by early humans that became lost during Earth's changes. It is where (on Earth) Source initially separated from Itself, creating the first step-down as the Lemurians and began the experiment of intentionally descending into lower dimensions to experience physicality. In Lemuria, the original expression of Source was free thought and free choice. Over time, Lemurians descended into physicality and lived in all dimensions.

Light

Light is divine energy, and as it emanates and moves in all directions, it is one of the guiding factors in our soul expansion, not just our consciousness, and may sometimes be called Spirit.

Lightworkers

Lightworkers are beings here to assist with the awakening in many different capacities. Like all humans, their blueprints are unique. Some are here to awaken first to reach a critical mass (the hundredth-monkey effect) and trigger global awakening. Others may be here to be a victim, an instigator, a healer, or even a villain. Lightworkers' actions inspire others to awaken, which can happen with some people playing many different roles. Some Lightworkers are Starseeds. See "Starseeds."

Magdalenes

The Magdalenes were a group of Essenes that included Mary Magdalene, Mother Mary, Yeshua, Miriam (Yeshua's cousin), Anna (Yeshua's grandmother), Sar'h, and others. This secretive group brought in a new awareness that one can experience one's higher self and sovereignty in physicality. The Magdalenes' DNA activated and moved forward through their children, impacting humanity.

Master Blueprint

The Master Blueprint is the Prime Creator's plan set at the beginning of the universe's creation, also called the Golden Age's master plan. The plan was for Source to experience physicality by descending the dimensions and returning to higher vibrations, lifting the world from duality into love and light.

Medium

See "psychic medium."

Multidimensionality

The soul or soul group is multidimensional, with other incarnations co-occurring in different dimensions or timelines. These multidimensional expressions are thought of as past, future, and present lives. These expressions include human, alien, angelic, elemental, animal, organic AI, and even matter.

Multiverse

The multiverse is multiple universes, also known as the omniverse, comprising all that exists: all space, time, matter, energy, and the physical laws and constants that define them. Some universes are parallel to each other and referred to as parallel universes, subsets of the multiverse. See "parallel lifetimes."

Myth

Mythology offers a metaphor to convey a fundamental understanding when no words or concepts explain the Truth thoroughly. It does not mean the myth is false; it provides a rudimentary expression of Truth. Humans can also empower the tale in consciousness with focused energy manifesting it into physicality.

New Children

Different generations of Starseeds have embodied to assist humanity's spiritual evolution. They are the Indigo Children, Crystal Children, Rainbow Children, Diamond Children, and Gold Children. See "Starseeds."

Indigo Children

Indigo Children are first-generation New Children. These people incarnated to bring about a new age of peace. Though not always, they were usually born throughout the late '70s to early '90s. They are typically sensitive, psychic, and here to cause a change in society, the environment, and government so that the Earth is a place of integrity. Often, they are labeled as rebels, troublemakers, and even problem children.

Crystal Children

Crystal Children are second-generation New Children. These children or individuals started coming in during the mid-nineties and are still incarnating. They are here to usher the world into the New Earth by showing how people can live in peace, kindness, and love. They are full of integrity and truth and often telepathic, though they may be seen as slow or autistic.

Rainbow Children

Rainbow Children are third-generation New Children. These Starseeds started arriving around the turn of the century. It is their first *earthly* incarnation, and they are here to generate unconditional love and play an essential role as they age. They are higher-dimensional beings who express pure love.

Diamond Children

Diamond Children are fourth-generation New Children, and some are first-timers on Earth. There is a small number of Diamond Children here. Adult New Children must evolve to birth the Diamond Children, who fully embody Divine Light. The Diamond Children possess the most advanced psychic skills, including telepathic communication and telekinesis. They are also instant manifesters.

The concepts of anger, hate, fear, greed, and separation are as foreign to Diamond Children as the concept of Oneness is to the majority of the planet during the 2020s. They resonate with Divine, Pure, Unconditional Love, the highest frequency. They hold the DNA patterning that awakens all

GODS IN THE GAME

those near them who are ready to overcome the illusion. They are walking healers. However, the Earth's frequency must elevate to accommodate a significant mass of incarnating Diamond People. The Ethereal Autists assist with this work.

Gold Children

The Gold Children are the newest generation of New Children. They began embodying around 2012 and are powerful energy conduits that help bring in and embody the new frequencies while harmonizing the old frequencies or energies. They have an X-code in their DNA structure, which includes a new metallic substance, gold strands entwined in the DNA structure. That metallic substance is reminiscent of liquid gold as it is soft, malleable, and Consciousness.

New Earth

The New Earth is the experience of the next evolutionary step for humanity. Humanity is on an evolutionary path of shifting from 3D to 5D.

Oneness

Oneness is the experience of being whole with the Universe, feeling connected with everything in existence at every level, including the higher self. Sometimes, it is called unity, Christ Consciousness, or enlightenment.

Parallel lifetimes

Undetectable universes exist in parallel and are subsets of the multiverse. We create alternate or parallel lifetimes anytime we put energy into deciding something. These alternate universes provide opportunities to maximize our life experiences. See "multiverse."

Psychic medium

A psychic medium is a specific type of psychic that mediates communication between individuals and spirits or other-dimensional entities. They may retain awareness of the events, whereas a trance medium generally goes into a trance, and when coming out of the trance, they are usually unaware of what occurred.

Polarity

Everything has an opposite: negative and positive, masculine and feminine, light and dark, action and reaction, and they attract each other. The two poles are complementary forces that work together to create a balance. Polarities occur so that Source can experience more of Itself. See "duality."

Pure Autists

Pure Autists (a.k.a. Autists) are a species that has existed on Earth since Lemuria. Today, many lightly connect to their physicality, which manifests in various ways, like communication disabilities. Nevertheless, they are far from disabled and have expanded consciousness. See "Ethereal Autists," "Catalytic Autists," and "Bridge Autists."

Serendipity

Serendipity is an event or situation that unfolds seemingly by accident or chance, which results in unexpected good, something beneficial, or a favorable outcome. It is the Universe's way of getting your attention and sending a sign to guide you.

Sovereign

Sovereign is the supreme power of having mastery of one's thoughts, emotions, beliefs, and perceptions and understands they have a choice and free will.

Sovereignty

Sovereignty is the power one has to be sovereign.

Starseeds

Starseeds incarnate in human form from other worlds, dimensions, and star systems and are often referred to as aliens. They walk among us as humans. Some may know they are aliens or Starseeds, while others are clueless. Starseeds are often Lightworkers serving in the spiritual evolution of the planet. The New Children and alien-human hybrids are Starseeds. As of 2023, approximately 3 percent of Earth's population is alien.

Synchronicity

Synchronicity is a meaningful coincidence orchestrated by the Universe to provide guidance, a message, or confirmation that one is on the right path. Each person can work with synchronicity to improve their life and guide them toward their Divine Blueprint.

Third dimension

The third dimension is the realm in which humankind lives, which is very dense and has a condensed consciousness. Each increasing level of dimension has rising awareness, frequency, and vibration.

Walk-in

The term walk-in is a soul exchange. It refers to a situation where a person's original soul, Spark of Life, departs their body (walks out) and is replaced with a new, often (but not always) more advanced soul. Sometimes, soul braiding occurs where either a higher aspect of the same soul or an advanced soul walks in, and both souls agree to occupy the same physical body for a higher purpose.

ABOUT THE CONTRIBUTORS

Connie

CONNIE was once skeptical until her son, Daniel, and his unique Autist pals opened her eyes to an unseen world. The Autists dared her to ask more questions to learn the Truth and be bold and brazen about sharing the gifts the Autist Collective has to bring to the world. She continues to learn and grow and is eager for the day when it is realized by all that we are One. Connie is a key contributor to *Gods in the Game* and *Destination New Earth* and served in many capacities, including being an intuitive and a conduit to her son's communications.

Daniel

DANIEL is a nonspeaking adult with autism who communicates using facilitated communication (FC), telepathy, and channeling.

GODS IN THE GAME

He works behind the scenes as a grid master of the ascension grid and is here to assist humanity in its evolutionary shift and heal the planet. He was instrumental in bringing to the world the messages of *Gods in the Game* and *Destination New Earth*.

Shauna Kalicki

SHAUNA KALICKI is a psychic medium that channels Cerian, a sixteenth-dimension collective, Ascended Masters, and Ethereal Autists. She is a certified empowerment coach, a Sacred Pipe Carrier, and a ceremonialist. She has traveled deep into the jungles of Peru, the temples of Bali, the caves and castles of France, and the mountains of Switzerland to open her energetic body to the frequencies of the Masters, awakening her innate abilities to channel their wisdom to help in humanity's evolution. Using her gifts, Shauna was instrumental in bringing to light much of the information in *Gods in the Game* and *Destination New Earth*.

Pictured from left to right, Daniel, Alex Marcoux,
Shauna Kalicki (rear) and Connie

ABOUT THE AUTHOR

ALEX MARCOUX is a multi-award-winning author of visionary fiction and spirituality books. She considers herself a truth-seeker as she has always sought truths hidden from humanity and woven them into her work, whether writing suspense or spiritual books. Since 2011, she has been on a journey, learning about the sacred mysteries and magic of autism and its relationship to humanity's spiritual evolution. Many of these truths are in Marcoux's *Gods in the Game, Destination New Earth*, and *The Unsuspected Heroes: A Visionary Fiction Novel.* Marcoux has seven books to date. Learn more about her at AlexMarcoux.com.

ENDNOTES

1   Alex Marcoux, *Destination New Earth*, (616 Editions an Imprint of Jenness Press, 2022), 94.

2   Marcoux, *Destination New Earth*, 33–34.

3   Marcoux, *Destination New Earth*, 77–78.

4   Marcoux, *Destination New Earth*, 154–155.

5   Marcoux, *Destination New Earth*, 202.

6   Marcoux, *Destination New Earth*, 67.

7   Metzger, "*The Text of the New Testament. Its Transmission, Corruption, and Restoration,*" (Oxford University Press), 195, 201.

8   Marcoux, *Destination New Earth*, 185.

9   Marcoux, *Destination New Earth*, 128.

10 Dr. Ananya Mandal, MD, "Autism History," *News Medical Life Sciences*, https://www.news-medical.net/health/Autism-History.aspx, Accessed 1/23/23.

11 A Primer on Cloning and Its Use in Livestock Operations https://public4.pagefreezer.com/browse/FDA/06-04-2023T20:24/https://www.fda.gov/animal-veterinary/animal-cloning/primer-cloning-and-its-use-livestock-operations, Accessed 11/28/23.

12 Wikipedia, Human cloning, https://en.wikipedia.org/wiki/Human_cloning, Accessed 3/26/23.

13 Scientists successfully create synthetic human fetus, *The Jerusalem Post*, https://www.jpost.com/science/article-746411, Accessed 11/28/23.

14 Wikipedia, Lee Carroll, https://en.wikipedia.org/wiki/Lee_Carroll#Channelings, Accessed 8/18/23.

15 Wikipedia, *The Law of One*, as published, https://shorturl.at/mwyR6, Accessed 1/29/23.

16 *The Law of One*, https://www.lawofone.info/books.php, Accessed 1/29/23.

17 *The Law of One People: Akhenaten*, https://www.lawofone.info/c/People?su=Akhenaten, Accessed 8/18/23.

Made in United States
Troutdale, OR
01/22/2024

17001459R00192